ONLINE POKER

STUART YARNOLD

BARNES & NOBLE BOOKS
NEW YORK

In easy steps is an imprint of Computer Step
Southfield Road · Southam
Warwickshire CV47 0FB · United Kingdom
www.ineasysteps.com

This edition published for Barnes & Noble Books, New York
FOR SALE IN THE USA ONLY
www.bn.com

Notice of Liability

Every effort has been made to ensure that this book contains accurate and
current information. However, Computer Step and the author shall not be
liable for any loss or damage suffered by readers as a result of any information
contained herein.

Acknowledgements and Trademarks

Thanks to PokerStars.com, PartyPoker.com and PacificPoker.com for allowing
the author to use images from their websites for illustrations in this book.
All trademarks are acknowledged as belonging to their respective companies.

Printed and bound in the United Kingdom

ISBN 0-7607-7855-8

Table of Contents

No-Limit Texas Hold'em

7

Tournaments

8

Omaha

9

Choosing Your Poker Room

Currently, there are some four hundred online poker rooms in operation. While most of them are above-board and offer a fair game to the player, there are some that don't, and thus should be avoided like the plague. Even some of the good ones have their negative aspects, and for any number of reasons may not be suitable for you.

This chapter explains everything you need to consider in order to find a poker room that you'll be comfortable in.

Covers

Chapter One

Introduction

As with casinos, online poker got off to a shaky start as many potential players were wary of being cheated by the site operators. There were also concerns regarding the safe handling of cash transactions. These were both valid concerns and, to an extent, still apply today. Players are advised to either stick to the well-known sites, or to check a site out thoroughly as described in this chapter.

The game of poker is unique in the requirements needed to play it successfully. A high level of knowledge, playing experience, endless patience, discipline, observation, and nerve are all needed. Add the element of playing for hard cash and we have the most compelling of all the many thousands of card games. No other game rewards the gambler as well for skillful play.

While its origins are unclear, it is thought that poker is descended from the Persian game of As Nas. The first direct reference to the game of poker in the USA shows its origins in New Orleans around 1830. Regardless of where it came from though, it is, and always has been, the most popular card game in America.

In its early days it was often played on riverboats, in smoke-filled back rooms and bars, and could be a dangerous activity with disputed hands settled "physically" on occasion. With the introduction of regulated casinos and poker rooms, it became a much more socially acceptable (and safer) pastime, and today is played regularly by some forty to fifty million people in the USA.

In the rest of the world, poker was not nearly so common, and in most countries it wasn't played at all. In England, people were more likely to be playing Cribbage and Whist; in Spain, they would be playing Brisca; in France, the game would be Bezique; and so on. Poker was, essentially, an American game.

The advent of the Internet and the subsequent introduction of online poker rooms has changed all this completely. All of a sudden, it was possible to play from anywhere in the world. The same reasons that made it so popular in America have made it popular in other world regions, now that it is available. While currently some fifty percent of online poker players are still American, this percentage is dropping all the time as the rest of the world scrambles to catch up. This explains the phenomenal growth of online poker.

The first online poker room was PlanetPoker, established in 1998, and swiftly followed in 1999 by ParadisePoker. It was not until 2000 and 2001 respectively, however, that the two most dominant online poker firms entered the fray – PokerStars and PartyPoker.

In 2003, the World Series of Poker Championship (WSOP) was won by a player who had never played in a bricks and mortar poker room – his skills were learned entirely from playing online. His prize was $2.5 million.

In 2003 PartyPoker launched a multi-million dollar marketing campaign that swiftly elevated it to the top of the online poker tree, a position it still holds today. Currently, this one site generates about half of the total revenue from online poker (at peak hours there will be between 17,000 and 22,000 people playing here).

In 2004, thanks in no small part to the success of PartyPoker and televised poker events, the game exploded on to the Internet with poker rooms opening up on an almost daily basis.

The monetary statistics are truly amazing. In 2004, some $1.5 billion was estimated to have been wagered in online poker rooms, half of it coming from the USA. This figure is expected to double in 2005 and possibly double again in 2006 as well. Worldwide, there are an estimated four million online players and rising.

The big winners, of course, are the site operators and the companies involved in writing the software. Probably ninety-nine percent of the players lose. The other one percent are the ones who have taken the time to learn how to play the game and, as a result, are in many cases making a handsome living from their online activities.

This brings us to the book. The reason that ninety-nine percent of players lose is that they don't know how to play poker properly, and also don't know how to exploit the advantages offered by online poker rooms. In the following pages we'll show you how to be in the one percent bracket – in other words, how to win.

In this book, you will find in-depth coverage of Texas Hold'em and Omaha Hi/Lo, plus the basics of Seven-Card Stud. We will also teach you how to win tournaments.

Please note that this is not a book on advanced poker theory. Our purpose here is first to introduce you to the world of online poker and show you how to exploit the advantages of playing online. Then we show you how to play the game.

Of the many versions of poker, Texas Hold'em is the most popular and so this is the one we will concentrate on. You'll learn how to play this game at a level that few of your online opponents will ever reach. We'll also teach you how to play Omaha, plus the rudiments of Seven-Card Stud.

Tournaments are a very popular manifestation of the online poker phenomenon and you'll discover how to triumph at these as well.

Bricks and Mortar versus Online

Online poker rooms are a completely different environment from bricks and mortar poker rooms. While the mechanics and strategy of the game are the same wherever you play, playing online does introduce some factors that won't be found in the traditional card room.

Hard Cash

In the online world, the dollar is king. With very few exceptions, all games are played in this currency.

Usually, in a bricks and mortar poker room you buy your chips with dollar bills. If you lose them, you have to hand over more dollar bills before you can get more chips. When you have no dollar bills left, you can't play anymore. You can, of course, use a credit card to get more chips, but by the time you've done this and gone back to the table, you've had time to think and may have second thoughts at the prospect of losing this as well. The fact that they're dealing with hard cash acts as a kind of "brake" to many people once they've lost a certain amount and stops them losing more than they can afford to.

In the online casino, however, there's no such thing as hard cash – the plastic card is king here – and all you see is numbers on a screen. When they have dwindled to zero, just click a few buttons and within a few seconds you're back in business. The sheer ease and speed with which you can deposit money in an online casino, plus the fact that you can't see or touch it, creates a mental disassociation that causes many people to lose sums of money online that they never would in a bricks and mortar casino.

Speed

In a traditional poker room there's not much else to do other than play poker.

In the comfort of your own home, however, you will be subject to many distractions. Keep these to the minimum as playing poker to win demands a high level of concentration.

Initially, the speed of online poker is bewildering (it is at least twice as fast as in a traditional poker room), so play a few hands at the free tables until you get used to it.

Also, because the games are so fast (50 or more hands an hour) you will be betting at least twice as much as you would in a bricks and mortar poker room in any given period. Bear this fact in mind when deciding what table limits to play: initially it might be prudent to play a lower limit than you would normally until you adjust to the speed of online play.

The element of speed also influences your actions at the table, for which you are allowed a specified length of time. Typically,

...cont'd

this is around 20 to 30 seconds. If you fail to act within that time, the software automatically folds your hand. Initially, this can be disconcerting and will take some getting used to.

Opponents

The most important difference, however, is the fact that you are completely isolated from your opponents; they could be aliens for all you know. This eliminates one of the most vital weapons in the good poker player's arsenal: being able to study opponents for any tell-tale signs of strength or weakness, and act accordingly. Many experienced players dislike playing online for this reason. For the inexperienced player, though, it's a definite advantage, and one less thing to have to think about.

Playing Options

Online poker rooms offer a huge range of tables at which to play. These range from the micro-limits at $0.05/0.10, up to the high-limits at $300/600. This gives you several advantages.

1) You are guaranteed to find a table that will suit your level of expertise. This is important for all but the very best players. Playing at a table where your opponents are at a more advanced level is the quickest way to go broke.

2) There will always be a table available at which the action is at a suitable level for your bankroll. This is also very important. Betting at limits that your bankroll can't sustain is another quick way to go broke.

3) You will have a huge number of players against whom to play. For example, if a particular player is beating you consistently then you can simply move to another table. You will also be able to go "fishing" (looking for weak opponents).

4) You have several hundred poker rooms to choose from. If you don't like one for some reason, then take your action to a different one.

Weighing it all up, the online poker room offers many advantages, particularly to the inexperienced player. Those brought up in the traditional bricks and mortar environment will find the inability to study opponents' body language a major disadvantage, though.

Because online poker doesn't alllow players to study the opposition, the beginner will have a much better chance against those more used to bricks and mortar card rooms. In this respect it has a definite "leveling off" effect.

"Limits" determine the size of the minimum bets at a table. In a game of Texas Hold'em there are four rounds of betting. The first two are at one level and the second two at a higher (twice the amount) level. So when you see a reference to a limit of $1.00/2.00, for example, this means that in the first two rounds of betting the minimum bet is $1 and in the second, it's $2.

Is Online Poker Legal?

As far as the player is concerned the answer to this question depends entirely on where in the world you live. In some countries it is, in some it isn't, and in others nobody seems to know for sure. For the poker rooms the issue is much more clear-cut.

USA

Currently, the laws applicable to online gambling are much more relevant to the site operators than they are to individual players.

The USA appears to fall into the latter category as there is no federal law that specifically addresses the issue of individuals gambling online. While the Internet Gaming Prohibition Act prevents casinos from running their operations within the US, it doesn't stop people from making online bets. However, the Justice Department is adamant that under the provisions of the Federal Wire Wager Act of 1961, online gambling is illegal. This is widely disputed though, and at the moment it is a very contentious issue. Most online players just ignore it and continue to play regardless. However, some individual states have specifically prohibited online gaming, so it would seem that the law is clear in some parts of the USA and ambiguous in others.

UK and Other Parts of the World

Players in the UK and much of Europe, South America, most of Asia, New Zealand, Mexico, most of the Caribbean, South Africa, and some other African countries are able to gamble online legally. Most countries will not allow online gaming sites to be located within their borders, though. However, many of the companies that run casinos offshore are actually operated from the USA – it is just their servers that are located offshore. This has led to the vast majority of gaming sites being established in a handful of countries, typically in the Caribbean and Pacific regions. Others include the Isle of Man, Alderney, Gibraltar, and Malta. Legislation is in the process of being passed that will allow gaming sites to be set up in the UK and could lead to this country soon being the location of choice.

Whether or not online poker is legal in your country, however, does seem to be somewhat academic, as the fact remains that due to the millions now engaged in this activity, any prohibitive laws that do exist are completely unenforceable. For example, regardless of state laws, millions of Americans gamble online illegally, but to date there is not one recorded case of someone being prosecuted.

Site Regulation

One of the most important things to look at when evaluating an online poker room is how the site is regulated and administered. Currently, there are well over 2000 casinos and several hundred poker rooms, and not all of them can be trusted to treat the player in a fair manner. Some are set up purely to fleece customers, others use software biased towards the casino, and still others deliberately withhold large payments.

Beware of sites that are unlicensed and do not follow the codes of conduct set by a watchdog organization.

However, it is a fact that most online gaming sites are reputable, and this is particularly the case with poker rooms. Remember, poker rooms have no vested interest in cheating their customers as they make their money from the "rake" that is taken from the pot at the end of each game. Whether players win or lose makes no difference to them – they always win.

Licensing

To satisfy players that they are offering a fair deal, sites pay large sums of money (typically, about $100,000 annually) for a license in the country in which they are registered. Under the terms of these licenses, the sites must allow themselves to be inspected periodically by the relevant government department in the licensing country.

There are quite a few watchdog organizations set up to monitor the online gaming industry. Three of the best known are:

- *Interactive Gaming Council – www.igcouncil.org*

- *Online Players Association – www.onlineplayersassociation. co.uk*

- *Gambling Commission – www.gamblingcommission.com*

Reputable sites will also be audited by one of the big international accounting firms, such as Price Waterhouse Coopers. Amongst other things checked is the site's random number generator. This is a program that generates a sequence of numbers that correspond to various cards, dice throws, roulette numbers, etc.

Regulatory Organizations

There is no legal obligation for any online gaming site to subject itself to regulation other than what's in the terms of its license – if it has one. If it hasn't, it can basically do what it likes. Reputable sites, however, follow codes of conduct set by watchdog organizations, such as the Interactive Gaming Council (IGC).

In essence then, online gaming is self-regulatory. Thus, you need to be careful. If you find a gaming site that isn't licensed and doesn't follow any codes of conduct, you have to ask yourself why.

Site Security

There are two issues to be considered here: firstly, how safe your financial details are, and secondly, how the site deals with players who cheat.

Financial Transactions

Basically, if you use an established poker room, you need have no worries on this point. Major sites spend millions of dollars on advertising to attract you to their site, and absolutely the last thing they want is to lose your business because of any financial irregularities. When this happens, word gets about very quickly, players desert in droves and the operators can go broke. To this end, they use extremely high-level data encryption methods, such as 128-bit SSL (Secure Socket Layer) Digital Encryption. This is the same level of protection as that offered by online banks and financial institutions, and is as safe as it gets – if you can't trust this, you can't trust anything.

To allow you to keep a close eye on your transactions, sites provide account histories. These are much the same as a bank statement and enable you to see exactly what's been taken out of, and paid into, your account.

Cheating

By this we mean players cheating other players. This can only occur at poker sites where players are pitted against each other (in casino games, such as blackjack or slots, the player is always pitted against the house).

As with bricks and mortar poker establishments, good online poker rooms take this issue very seriously and have made it all but impossible to do. About the only way it can be done is by player collusion, where two or more players communicate with each other by telephone or instant messaging in order to gain an unfair advantage. However, good sites do have systems in place which alert them when players do this. Furthermore, high-limit games are usually monitored by an observer for any signs of unusual or improper behavior.

Less reputable poker rooms probably couldn't care less about players cheating each other as long as they are getting their percentage, which is another reason to choose your site carefully.

Poker Room Software

While all poker software does the same thing (enables you to play poker), some are definitely better than others. You need to consider the following:

While not strictly a software issue, a site that drops your connection frequently due to problems with its servers is as bad as one that uses buggy software. Check this out by playing the free tables for a while, or looking in the online poker forums.

Aesthetics

This is probably the least important consideration but as you're going to be spending hours looking at it, you may as well like what you see in terms of the layout and graphics.

Functionality

When you're sitting there with a hand full of aces and kings and opponents are betting into you, the last thing you need is for a buggy piece of software to stop responding or to freeze your PC. Unfortunately, this sort of thing does happen and can be infuriating (not to mention being extremely costly). This type of problem is much less likely with the well established poker sites, such as PartyPoker, that use tried-and-tested software. However, if you're trying out an unknown site, play at the free tables for a while or stick to the micro-limit tables until you're satisfied on this point.

Software Options

Not all poker software provides the player with the same options and features. Examples are note-taking facilities, viewing options (large, medium or minimized table size), and downloading of hand histories to the player's PC. These are all worth having.

Another very useful feature to look out for is session statistics. As you play at the tables, statistics of all your actions are kept and are instantly available. This allows you to analyze your play in real-time (to a limited extent), or after your poker session. An example from PokerStars is shown below.

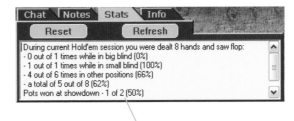

Your session statistics

Cashing in Your Chips

Five sites with good reputations for prompt handling of cash-outs are: PokerStars, PartyPoker, Ladbrokes, UltimateBet, and ParadisePoker.

This is what it's all about – winning, cashing in, and switching off the PC with a smug grin. Sadly though, no poker room will ever give you your money with the same alacrity with which it takes it. While they will pay out eventually, the speed at which they do so varies considerably. This issue is one of the biggest grouches players have with online poker sites.

Some sites have better cash-out procedures than others. The best ones handle your cash-out request promptly and with no delaying tactics. This usually means a 1-3 day wait on your first cash-out request while they do some anti-fraud checks. Subsequent withdrawals will usually be handled more quickly. Once the withdrawal has been approved, some additional time may be required depending on the cash-out method. Neteller takes only a few seconds, an electronic funds transfer two or three days, a mailed bank draft a week or more.

So how can you, the player, tell which poker rooms have a quick cash-out policy and which don't? Most will tell you their policy when you click the software's Withdrawal option. However, relying on this is akin to believing a politician's promises: you really need something more concrete.

One way is to deposit the minimum amount, immediately cash it out and see how long it takes to reappear in your account. However, this doesn't cover the possibility that the site will deliberately drag its heels on large withdrawals only – and some do. (Usually, in this situation, they will cite the need for security and may even demand to see proof of identity. If you live in Poland and the site is based in Belize, you can envisage the problems you may have.)

So, the Internet is where you go. Here you will get feedback on all casinos and poker rooms. If you can't find much information on the site in question, be immediately suspicious. Also, check the websites of the various gaming watchdogs and take a look at their lists of blacklisted casinos and poker rooms. Poker user forums are another good source of information.

Deposit and Withdrawal Options

Online Transfer Services

There are quite a few companies providing an online money transfer service. Basically, they are a holding house with whom you set up an account. Money is transferred to the account from your bank or credit card, and is then available for deposit into your poker room account. Of these, Neteller is generally reckoned to be the best. It is supported by virtually all the poker rooms and provides a large number of deposit and withdrawal options, including several instant transfer methods. Other companies include FirePay, Central Coin, and Citadel.

Of all the various money transfer methods, Neteller is one of the most useful. Virtually all online gaming sites accept it, and it can also be used for general Internet shopping.

Western Union

Western Union handles most forms of payment, such as credit cards. It can also be used to deposit hard cash (this must be taken to a Western Union office); this is handy if you don't have a bank account or credit card. However, only a few poker rooms support Western Union.

Credit and Debit Cards

These used to be the usual method but for various reasons, the credit card companies, notably MasterCard and Visa, are no longer so keen to deal with online gaming sites. It is virtually impossible to make a deposit with MasterCard now, and Visa is making it increasingly difficult. Bank debit cards are usually OK.

Note that most of the companies providing online transfer services restrict their operations to holders of US bank accounts. Neteller, however, provides an international service.

Phone Connect Cards

These are prepaid phone cards and work in the same way as a prepaid credit card. They can be purchased and activated using Visa, MasterCard, Amex, Discover, Diners Club International, Switch, Solo, and JCB. They are increasingly supported by poker rooms.

Bank Wire Transfer

This is an electronic transfer of funds from your bank account to your poker room account and usually takes between one and four days. Transaction charges can be high, depending on your bank.

Personal Checks

This is the slowest method of all and it can take anything up to ten days before the money is credited to your account. Some poker rooms are reluctant to accept this deposit method.

Site Support

Assuming everything works as it should and you never have a problem, site support is not something you will ever need. However, play at any one site long enough and something is bound to crop up eventually. Problems do occur, even with the best sites, and when they do it's essential that you have some means of contacting the site's operators quickly (quickly being the operative word). Unfortunately, as with cashing-out, this is an area in which far too many poker rooms offer an unacceptable level of service.

Some sites provide little, or no, customer support. An email link may be there and telephone numbers may be provided, but they either don't respond at all, or take their own sweet time in doing so.

This is an issue that you ignore at your own risk. If money goes missing from your account or you have problems cashing-out, and you are unable to contact the site's operators, you are going to find yourself with very few options.

So before you trust a site with your money, check out its customer support. Send them an email saying you can't figure out how to make a deposit. If they don't respond to that immediately then what chance have you got when you have a problem withdrawing money? – move on swiftly. Ring the support telephone number and see how long it takes them to answer. If they don't answer at all – again, move on. Try ringing them at an unsociable hour – good sites have customer support available 24 hours a day, seven days a week. Remember, online sites are used by players from all time zones.

The level of customer support offered is also a good indicator of how professional a site's operators are in general. If they've got this aspect buttoned down, it's quite likely that everything else will be run equally well.

A typical example of when you might need to contact a site is with regard to bonuses. Some sites set onerous and difficult to understand qualifying conditions for these. You may think you've qualified for a particular bonus and then be puzzled when it isn't credited to your account. Obviously, you'll need to find out why.

The Rake

While, in general, all the poker rooms have similar rake levels, by "shopping around", you may be able to find a site offering a better deal in this respect at the limits you play. It may not make much difference in the short term, but in the long term, it will.

The rake is what it's all about as far as the poker rooms are concerned – this is how they make their money (and how you lose some of yours). On every single game, they take a percentage of the pot. Typically, at the low-limit tables this is 5%, rising in increments of $0.25 to a cap (maximum) of between $1 and $3. Put another way (and assuming a cap of $3) this means that if the pot is $60, then they take $3 (5% of $60 is $3). If the pot is larger than $60, the rake is still $3 due to the cap.

Now you might be thinking that all the poker rooms must take the same rake as no one is going to play at one that takes a higher rake than the others. In fact, you'd be completely wrong. We're not going to mention names here as certain sites may object to being shown in a negative light. As a typical example, though, at the $0.50/1.00 tables with an average pot of $5, one well known site (which we'll call Site A) has a rake of 10%, while another well known site (site B) has a rake of 5%. To demonstrate the effect of this, we'll do some simple math.

The cost-effectiveness of online poker rooms is highlighted by the fact that the rake is usually half that found in bricks and mortar poker rooms.

You play 2 hours a day for a month = 60 hours.
You play 50 hands an hour = 3000 hands.
You win 1 hand in 10 = 300 winning hands.

The average pot is $5 so you win $1500 (300 x 5).
At site A the rake is 10% = $150 taken by the poker room.
At site B the rake is 5% = $75 taken by the poker room.

By playing this table limit at site B you will be $75 a month better off than you would have been playing at site A. Over a year that stacks up to a cool $900. Over ten years you've saved $9000.

All good poker rooms make their rake charts available to players. Any that don't should be avoided as they could be taking an extortionate amount out of each pot you win.

The cap (as explained above) can also make a big difference. If sites A and B both have a rake of 10%, but A has a cap of $3 while B has a cap of $1: on a $30 pot, site A will be raking $3 while site B will be raking $1 – a 66% difference.

Millions of players never give the rake a thought and, as a result, over a period of time may be losing much more than they should be. Most poker rooms publish a rake chart. All you have to do is compare them at the limits you intend to play and choose the one offering the lowest rake and/or cap.

Bonuses

Online poker sites are spreading like wildfire and they all want a slice of your cash. While bricks and mortar poker rooms offer players free meals, drinks, and rooms as incentives, online poker rooms have only one thing to give you – hard cash. Needless to say though, there are catches involved. So let's take a look at what's on offer (and the catches).

Sign-Up Bonuses

If a particular site's sign-up bonus gets your attention, be sure to read the small print before giving them your money. Some sites make it very difficult to actually earn the bonus.

To lure players into their sites, casinos and poker rooms offer a sign-up bonus. These vary according to the site, but usually they will be up to a maximum of $100 depending on the size of the initial deposit. At PartyPoker, for example, the bonus is 20%. So to get the $100 you must deposit $500. Over at PacificPoker, the bonus is 25%, so to get the $100 you need only deposit $400.

An even better deal is on offer at UltimateBet – a 40% sign-up bonus up to $200. Deposit $500 to get $200, $250 to get $100, etc.

This all sounds wonderful but, unfortunately, there is a snag as you'll discover if you try and cash-out your bonus immediately – the poker room won't let you. To be able to claim your bonus, you must first "earn it", and this involves staking a specified amount of cash, or playing a specified number of raked hands. This gives the poker room an opportunity to get some (if not all) of the bonus back. For example, one of them demands that you wager 20 times the bonus amount ($2000 to get the maximum bonus of $100). Some also specify a time limit, whereby you will need to play a certain number of raked hands within a specified period.

Loyalty Bonuses

In our opinion good loyalty bonuses are worth far more than sign-up bonuses. In the long term, they will earn you much more money.

Having got your business, the poker rooms want to keep it; they don't want you taking your money elsewhere. To this end, they offer loyalty bonuses. The more you wager and play with a poker room, the higher your loyalty rating will be. Some pay on-going bonuses according to the amounts you deposit. Others give bonuses on a weekly or monthly basis. For example, William Hill in the UK gives you $25 every month ($5 for each of the first five hours of play).

The bonus details described on these pages were correct at the time of going to press. However, they may well have changed by the time you are reading this. Our purpose here is just to give you an idea of what's on offer.

Generally, these bonuses have conditions attached, similar to those for sign-up bonuses; you will have to gamble them a number of times before you can cash them in.

Other Bonuses

There are any number of these, and as with the loyalty bonuses, are well worth looking out for. A typical example here is the happy hour bonus. Make a deposit between, say, 10:00 pm and midnight, and you'll receive a free $10 chip.

Another method of rewarding players is by awarding them points. This can be based on numerous factors, such as number of hands played, playing at a certain limit, depositing certain amounts, etc. These points can be converted into cash or used as buy-ins for tournaments.

High rollers are rewarded for staking large sums. These bonuses range from $100 to $500.

Most poker rooms award jackpots for hitting a royal flush (the best poker hand possible), and bad-beats (the best losing hand). These jackpots are often progressive and increase by a certain amount each day until a lucky player qualifies.

Bonus Players

These are players who play only for the sign-up bonuses. As soon as they've earned one, they cash it in and move on to another site.

If you play for the bonuses only, the poker rooms will soon realize what you're up to and put a stop to it.

This is a very common practice of which the casinos and poker rooms are well aware. While it's perfectly legal and above board, needless to say they are not enamoured with it.

If you decide to do this yourself, be aware that there is a blacklist circulating around the sites containing the names of known bonus players. If you happen to be on this list, you will find that many sites will simply refuse to pay you the bonus. Obviously, you will be able to do it a number of times before they catch on to you, but if you overdo it, you will eventually find yourself blacklisted.

Five Top Poker Rooms

PartyPoker

In terms of revenue, this is the largest poker room in the world. Very popular and with an excellent reputation, PartyPoker is licensed in Gibraltar, and is a member of the Interactive Gaming Council.

Website: www.partypoker.com.

Traffic
Cash game traffic reaches 20,000 people at peak periods. Tournament traffic is up to 23,000.

Games Hosted
Texas Hold'em, Omaha, Omaha Hi/Lo, Seven-Card Stud, and Seven-Card Stud Hi/Lo.

Lobby

Table Limits
Lowest limit is $0.50/1.00. Highest limit is $100/200.

Software
The graphics are nice and the software is fast and reliable.

Competition
Due to the huge number of players here, there are easy pickings to be found at this site. You can find weak players even at the middle-limit tables. If you can't win here, you won't win anywhere.

Cash Transfer
Deposit options are: VISA, MasterCard, Diners Club, debit cards, FPS-ePassport, phone connect cards, Western Union, Neteller, European Union bank transfers, wire transfers, Moneybookers, and personal checks.

Table

Cash-out options are: debit cards, Neteller, FPS-ePassport, personal checks, and Moneybookers.

Customer Support
24/7 telephone support with a quick response time. Email support is good. PartyPoker also provides live 24/7 floor person support.

Security
As good as will be found anywhere.

PacificPoker

This site has grown rapidly over the last couple of years and is now a favorite haunt for many players. It is licensed in Gibraltar and is a member of the Interactive Gaming Council.

Website: www.pacificpoker.com.

Website

Traffic
Cash game traffic is up to 2500 at peak times.
Tournament traffic is up to 5000.

Games Hosted
Texas Hold'em, Omaha, Omaha Hi/Lo, Seven-Card Stud, and Seven-Card Stud Hi/Lo.

Table Limits
The lowest limit is $0.05/0.10 (good for beginners) and the highest is $30/60.

Lobby

Software
Graphics are nice and all the usual features are available.

Competition
This site is generally considered to be one of the easiest sites to play at in terms of the quality of the opposition.

Cash Transfer
Deposit options include: VISA, MasterCard, Diners Club, Eurocard, FirePay, debit cards, ACTeCASH, Neteller, ePassporte, bank transfers, personal checks, wire transfers, and PrePaidATM.

Table

Cash-out options are: debit cards, FirePay, Neteller, PrePaidATM, wire transfers, and bank drafts.

Customer Support
Email and telephone response is reasonable. No live support is provided, though.

Security
Appears to be good with no reported issues.

UltimateBet

Established in 2000, UltimateBet is a very slick and professional operation that is licensed by the Kahnawake Gaming Commission in Canada. It is known for its fast payouts.

A useful feature offered by UltimateBet is the mini-view. This reduces the size of the game window and allows players to have up to four separate tables in full view simultaneously. This is very useful for those who play multiple tables (see page 165).

Website: www.ultimatebet.com.

Traffic
Cash game traffic reaches 3000 at peak times. Tournament traffic reaches 3600.

Games Hosted
Texas Hold'em, Omaha, Omaha Hi/Lo, Seven-Card Stud, Seven-Card Stud Hi/Lo, Crazy Pineapple, and Lowball.

Table Limits
For the high roller, UltimateBet features some of the highest limit games on the Internet at $300/600. However, it also goes to the opposite extreme with limits as low as $0.10/0.20.

Software
This is one of the site's best features. Quick and reliable, it is also great to look at. Players have a choice of five different backgrounds. An advanced statistics function is available.

Competition
There are easier sites at which to play. Overall, playing standards are high.

Cash Transfer
Deposit options are: VISA, MasterCard, Neteller, FirePay, Citadel, debit cards, and bank drafts.

Cash-out options are: Neteller, FirePay, debit cards, and personal checks.

Customer Support
The only support provided is email. However, the response time is excellent.

Security
Appears to be good with no reported issues.

InterPoker is part of the Cryptologic network. Other sites using the Cryptologic software are:

- *Caribbean Sun*
- *Littlewoods Poker*
- *William Hill*
- *Ritz Club London*

InterPoker

Established in 2001, and licensed in Cyprus, InterPoker is one of the fastest-growing poker rooms (400% growth in 2004). Games can be played in dollars, sterling or Euros.

Website: www.interpoker.com.

Traffic
Cash game traffic is up to 2000 at peak times with a similar figure for tournaments.

Games Hosted
Texas Hold'em, Omaha, Omaha Hi/Lo, and Seven-Card Stud.

Table Limits
The lowest limit is $0.25/0.50 and the highest is $150/300. The same limits apply for those playing in sterling.

Software
The graphics are nice, and the level of features, such as player statistics, is good.

Competition
Not too difficult. Reasonable players will more than hold their own here.

InterPoker is another site that rewards players with points. These can be earned by registering an account, playing cash games and tournaments.

Cash Transfer
Deposit options are: VISA, MasterCard, debit cards, ECP, personal checks, Citadel, FirePay, Neteller, and wire transfers.

Cash-out options are: debit cards, ECP, personal checks, Citadel, Neteller, FirePay, and wire transfers.

Customer Support
Live online, telephone, and email support are provided.

Security
No problems here.

PokerStars

PokerStars is one of the older and more established poker rooms, having been around since 2000. After PartyPoker, it is the second largest poker room. The site is registered in Costa Rica.

Website: www.pokerstars.com.

Website

Traffic
For cash games, traffic levels peak at about 5000. Tournament traffic is much higher, typically 25,000 players. This makes PokerStars the most popular poker room for tournaments.

Games Hosted
Texas Hold'em, Omaha, Omaha Hi/Lo, Seven-Card Stud, and Seven-Card Stud Hi/Lo.

Table Limits
This site features some of the lowest limits on the Internet at $0.04/0.08. The highest limit is $30/60.

Lobby

Software
Fast and reliable. The graphics are nice and the level of statistical information provided is good.

Competition
This is not a poker room for beginners as the standard of competition is tough. This is particularly so in the tournaments.

Cash Transfer
Deposit options are: VISA, MasterCard, Neteller, FirePay, and CentralCoin.

Table

Cash-out options are: Neteller, FirePay, CentralCoin, and personal checks.

Customer Support
PokerStars only provides email support. However, the response time is very good.

Security
As with all the major sites, security is excellent.

Getting to Grips With Poker Software

The purpose of this chapter is to make sure you know and understand all the important poker room features, and how to use them to your advantage.

The rules of the game itself will be explained in later chapters. Here, we are just introducing the software.

Covers

The Poker Room Lobby

Having logged on to your poker room, the first thing you will see is the lobby. This is the control center of the poker room and gives you access to all the games, plus various options and features.

In some poker lobbies, you can expand the table list to show all the available limits, as shown below.

Choosing and Accessing a Table

We'll demonstrate this with the lobby at PokerStars, which is typical of all poker room lobbies.

1   At the top are all the games on offer at the poker room. Click the one you want to play, and in the middle you will be shown a complete list of the tables where that game is being played

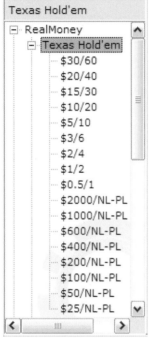

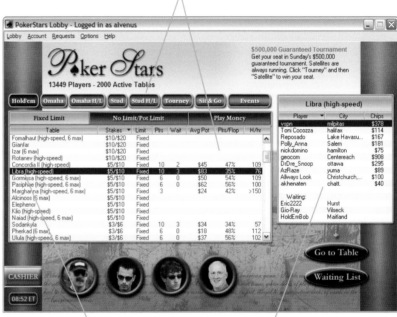

This saves you having to search through the complete list of tables.

2   Highlight a table, and at the right you will see the screen aliases of the players seated there. If you wish to join it press the Go to Table button. If the table is fully occupied, press the Waiting List button to enter the queue. When a seat becomes available you will be notified. In the meantime, you can browse the site or play at another table

Lobby Options

Most of these are self-explanatory and we won't go into each and every one of them. Instead, we'll just look at three that we consider to be particularly useful.

Hand Histories

One of the best ways to improve your game is to compile statistics of your playing sessions, which can be analyzed afterwards (see pages 163-164). Good poker software helps you to do this by enabling you to download session statistics to your PC in the form of hand histories. Some poker clients, such as the one used by PartyPoker, actually do this automatically; with others, you have to request the hand histories to be sent by email.

Buddy List

The buddy list provides a convenient way of recording the screen names of players that you may want to find in a subsequent session. It also tells you which players in the list are currently active.

Player Search

There are any number of reasons why you might want to find a particular player. You may have enjoyed playing against this player, you may have struck up a friendship via the chat facility, or this may be an easy-to-beat player. Whichever, by using the software's Player Search facility, you will be able to locate the table at which the player is seated (assuming he or she is playing, of course).

1 Enter the player you want to locate and then click Find

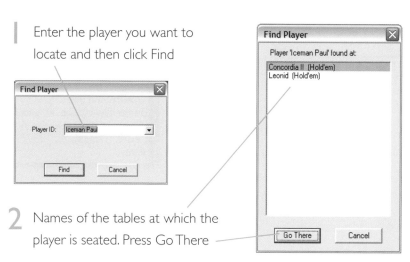

2 Names of the tables at which the player is seated. Press Go There

The Poker Table

The rake

10   The player's alias

9   Your hand. The figure beneath is the size of your stack

8   Automatic action controls

7   Type your chat here and press Enter

2 The community cards

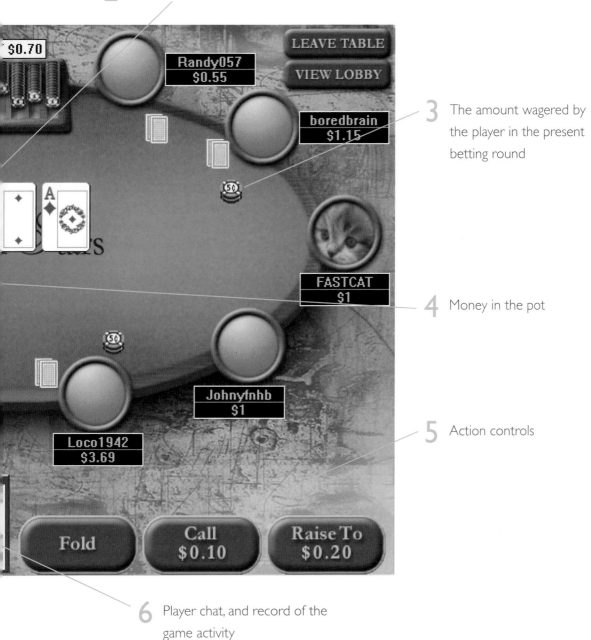

$0.70

LEAVE TABLE

VIEW LOBBY

Randy057
$0.55

boredbrain
$1.15

3 The amount wagered by
the player in the present
betting round

A

FASTCAT
$1

4 Money in the pot

Johnyfnhb
$1

Loco1942
$3.69

5 Action controls

Fold

Call
$0.10

Raise To
$0.20

6 Player chat, and record of the
game activity

Poker Table Options

As you can see from pages 30-31, there are various features and options provided by an online poker table. We'll look at these in a bit more detail.

Action Controls

These buttons control your actions at the table and vary according to the type of game you are playing.

In a fixed-limit game, when it's your turn to make a move, you will see the following options:

| Check | Fold | Call $0.50 | Raise To $1 |

Stay in the game without making a bet — Discard your hand — Match a previous player's bet — Call the previous bet and raise it

After you've made a bet, a different set of options will be available:

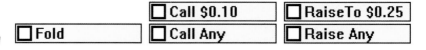

☐ Fold   ☐ Call $0.10   ☐ RaiseTo $0.25   ☐ Call Any   ☐ Raise Any

If you check any of these options, the software will automatically carry out the instruction if it's available when it's your turn to play. This is useful if you need to answer the door or the telephone in the middle of a hand, for example.

In a no-limit or pot-limit game, you are provided with an option that allows you to choose the size of the bet yourself – there is no restriction as in a fixed-limit game.

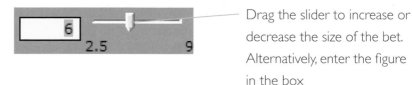

Drag the slider to increase or decrease the size of the bet. Alternatively, enter the figure in the box

Automatic Action Controls

Typically, you will have four options here. The first, "Fold to any bet" is clear enough. By checking the second, "Auto Post Blind",

the software will automatically post the blinds bets (see top margin note). Checking "Muck Losing/Uncalled Hands" will prevent these hands being revealed to other players at the end of a game. The final option, "Deal Me Out", allows you to sit out a few hands without sacrificing your position at the table.

The blinds (small blind and big blind) are forced bets that each player must make in turn. The purpose is to ensure there is always money in the pot and that players don't simply wait until they have the top hand before they make a bet.

Player Location

Almost all poker software allows you to see where your opponents are in the world. To do this just hover the pointer over the player's alias.

Player Notes

An important part of playing poker successfully is knowing your opponents. If you play regularly at a particular poker room, you will, inevitably, run into players more than once. You will probably

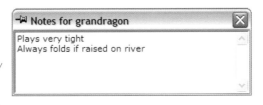

remember their alias but not the way they play. By right-clicking a player, you will be able to open a Notes window that allows you to make pertinent

Most poker software will show you the strength of your hand, e.g. a pair of nines, or a full house. Find out where this is and refer to it constantly. It's all too easy to misread the cards, particularly if you're tired or have been playing for a long period.

comments that may be useful should you meet again. These are saved automatically by the software.

Game Activity Record

This is a sequential record of every move made by each player in every hand. It is a very useful reference tool that you can use to check previous hands. Player chat (see next page) also appears here.

Iceman Paul: na
Bluesman: I folded 72
Dealer: Game #2245184274: m8675309a wins pot ($50)
Iceman Paul: Ive been calling with good hands (expect the one I slaughtered you on) .. Medics just been killing me on the draw
Dealer: Game #2245186820: Ubstr811 wins pot ($10)

Player Chat

Poker software provides an instant chat facility that enables players to converse with each other. This makes use of the game activity window.

It's entirely up to you whether you use the chat facility. However, poker players are generally a friendly bunch of people, and some good-natured banter can make the game much more enjoyable.

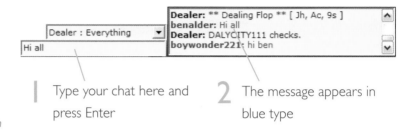

| 1 | Type your chat here and press Enter | 2 | The message appears in blue type |

The table below shows a list of commonly used chat abbreviations.

A word of warning: take absolutely no notice of what anyone might say regarding the strength of their hand in the middle of a game. Online players will use whatever means are available in order to gain an edge – this includes the chat facility.

brb	Be right back	sete	Smiling ear to ear
b4n	Bye for now	sys	See you soon
fc	Fingers crossed	tks	Thanks
gg	Good game	tx	Thanks
gga	Good game all	ty	Thank you
gl	Good luck	ul	Unlucky
gp	Good play	vn	Very nice
gmab	Give me a break	vnh	Very nice hand
gtg	Got to go	vul	Very unlucky
hig	How's it going	vwp	Very well played
lol	Laugh out loud	wb	Welcome back
nl	Nice one	wd	Well done
nh	Nice hand	wp	Well played
np	No problem	yhs	Your hand sucks
omg	Oh my God	yw	You're welcome

Note that if you misuse the chat facility by sending obscene or otherwise unpleasant messages, the poker room will prevent you from using it.

Choosing Your Poker Game and Table

A very important, but much overlooked, aspect of online poker is playing the right game at the right table. This applies particularly to beginners for whom the wrong choice can be devastating. However, if you make the right choice your chances of winning increase considerably.

This chapter explains all the factors you need to consider in order to find a profitable table.

Chapter Three

Covers

Choosing the Right Type of Game

Throughout the next three chapters we are going to concentrate on Texas Hold'em. Online poker rooms offer three variations of this game: fixed-limit, no-limit and pot-limit. The rules are the same for each; the difference lies in the betting structure.

For the beginner, making the correct choice here is crucial, and this section will show you why.

The action at no-limit tables is fast and furious, and it is possible to win (and lose) a lot of money very quickly. For these reasons, many good poker players play no-limit exclusively. For the inexperienced player, they are a minefield that should be given a wide berth.

No-Limit Games

No-limit poker means just what the name implies – you can bet whatever you like up to the amount in front of you. Because of this, it is possible to lose your entire stack in a single hand if you make the wrong call. The following example illustrates the danger of this type of game.

You sit down with $20 at a $0.50/1.00 no-limit table thinking you should be fairly safe at such a low-level game. The game proceeds and no one is making any monster bets. You get off to a good start and relax. After three hours you're up to $75 and are feeling good.

All-in is when a player puts his or her entire stack in the pot. See page 108 for more on this.

Then it happens. You hit an ace set (three aces) and raise by $15. All your opponents fold with the exception of Player A who re-raises by $20. You respond by calling; now you have $35 in the pot. On the next round of betting, you bet $10 and player A raises you by $30. To see A's cards, you now have to go all in (see Hot Tip).

You have three aces, which is a very good hand but not one that's unbeatable. If you call, you have a good chance of winning. If you lose, though, you will have lost your entire stack in one hand. If you fold, you lose the $45 you have already staked. The former is a catastrophe, the latter is a minor catastrophe. An even bigger catastrophe, however, will be folding the winning hand. In this case, you'll have lost a pot that's worth well over $100.

This is a very tricky situation and demands that you get your next move right. An experienced player will know how to handle the dilemma. A beginner, though, will probably chicken out and simply take the easy option of folding, which could well be a major mistake. It's better not to get yourself involved in this type of scenario at all by avoiding no-limit to begin with.

This situation is one that will crop up time and time again if you play no-limit poker and is the main reason that inexperienced players should avoid it completely.

Pot-Limit Games

Pot-limit games are the same as no-limit, apart from a slight variation in the betting structure.

Pot-limit games are very similar to no-limit games. The only difference is that players can bet no more than the amount in the pot. For example, say there is $20 in the pot after one round of betting. The player opening the second round may bet any amount up to $20. If he or she does bet $20, making a pot of $40, the next player may call the first player's bet ($20) and then raise the amount of the current pot, including the call ($60), for a total bet of $80.

In the early betting rounds, therefore, where the pot will be small, the danger of being faced with a monster bet to stay in the game is much reduced. However, in a game where the betting is heavy, the pot size will increase rapidly and, consequently, so will the maximum bet allowed.

For the beginner, the dangers inherent in pot-limit poker are much the same as in no-limit. It should, therefore, be avoided.

Fixed-Limit Games

All players new to poker are advised to start at fixed-limit tables as the risk of sustaining heavy losses in a short period is much less. Furthermore, you are much more likely to be playing against weak opponents.

In fixed-limit poker, all bet sizes are pre-determined. For example, all bets during the first two rounds of a $5.00/10.00 Texas Hold'em game are in increments of $5 ($5 being the minimum bet). If Jim bets $5 then John can fold, call for $5, or raise to $10. In the last two betting rounds, the minimum bet is $10 and bets rise in increments of $10.

Something else to be aware of is that most poker rooms limit the number of raises during any betting round in Texas Hold'em to four. This includes a bet, raise, re-raise, and cap. The cap is the third and final raise. After a betting round is capped, players still in the game only have the option to call or to fold.

These games are much safer for the beginner as there is no danger of being faced with a huge bet.

Therefore, fixed-limit games are the ones recommended for those new to the game of poker.

Choosing the Right Table

Experienced players consider several factors before sitting down at a table. This is because they know that if they pick the right one, their chances of walking away with a pocketful of cash at the end of the session will be substantially higher.

If good players feel the need to do this, then it is even more imperative that beginners do the same. However, they rarely do. This is just one of the many reasons that these players lose consistently.

So before you place your chips on a table, we are going to show how to choose one at which you have a good chance of winning.

Average Pot versus Stack

You must have an adequate amount of money (your stack) in relation to the average pot at the table. For example, if you sit down with $10 at a table where the average pot is $50, you are likely to experience the following:

1) You hit a monster hand at the same time that one or two other players also get good hands that they are prepared to bet on to the end. Because you only have $10, you will be all in very early in the game. Meanwhile, the others will continue to bet in another pot. When the showdown comes, although you've got the best hand, you will only win the pot that you were involved in. The other pot (that will contain most of the money) will go to the player with the next best hand. You will have missed a golden opportunity to win a large pot with a virtually unbeatable hand.

2) In an effort to avoid busting-out, you will play ultra-cautiously. In doing so, you may well pass up good winning opportunities in your determination to stay in the game. In other words, you're compromising yourself.

3) Your opponents will play differently against you. They will try to take advantage by calling and raising your bets, knowing you haven't got enough to hurt them if you do win a hand.

This leads us to the question of how much you should have for the limits at which you intend to play. Basically, you need to have sufficient to cover a long losing streak and still have enough left to enable you to maximize the winnings should you turn up a monster hand, and also to play confidently in general without compromising your strategy.

All tables have a minimum and maximum buy-in amount. For example: $20 minimum, $100 maximum. Ideally, you would sit down with the maximum amount – $100, or $50 at least.

Quality of the Opposition

This is the most important factor of all. Quite simply, if you get this right you should win; get it wrong and you'll probably lose. You can determine this as follows:

Before joining a table, watch how the hands are being played. What you are looking for is a table with several players who bet on most hands. Even better are players who are constantly raising. People who play like this are usually betting on poor hands in the hope of hitting a lucky card. Play the right strategy (see Chapter 6) against players of this type and you will beat them. Tight players who fold most hands are no-risk types who will be more difficult to beat.

A quicker way of establishing how "tight" or "loose" a table is can be found in the poker room lobby. An example from PokerStars is shown below.

If you find yourself becoming short-stacked, top it up. You must keep it at a level that will enable you to make the most of situations where you have the best hand and opponents are betting into you.

In poker, the term "tight" is used to describe players who play very cautiously. A tight table, therefore, will be one full of tight players. A "loose" player is the opposite: one who plays recklessly.

Fixed Limit		No Limit/Pot Limit			Play Money		
Table	Stakes ▼	Limit	Plrs	Wait	Avg Pot	Plrs/Flop	H/hr
Mora (6 max)	$10/$20	Fixed					
Sekanina (high-speed, 6 max)	$10/$20	Fixed					
Circinus II (high-speed)	$5/$10	Fixed	10	2	$53	33%	72
Halaesus	$5/$10	Fixed	10	1	$69	71%	102
Hynek (high-speed)	$5/$10	Fixed	10	2	$54	35%	83
Liriope	$5/$10	Fixed	10	1	$56	21%	83
Procyon II	$5/$10	Fixed	10	2	$50	25%	66
Alphard IV (high-speed, 6 max)	$5/$10	Fixed	6	0	$49	55%	73
Gefion (high-speed, 6 max)	$5/$10	Fixed	6	0	$40	42%	144
Meyer (high-speed, 6 max)	$5/$10	Fixed	6	0	$55	51%	102
Izar II (6 max)	$5/$10	Fixed	5		$47	47%	100
Clorinde (high-speed)	$5/$10	Fixed					
Delvaux	$5/$10	Fixed					
Naantali (high-speed, 6 max)	$5/$10	Fixed					
Octans II (6 max)	$5/$10	Fixed					
Ausonia	$3/$6	Fixed	10	1	$30	33%	76

Not all poker rooms provide players with the flop percentages.

Look at the Plrs/Flop column, which will tell you the percentage of the players who bet through to the flop (the first three community cards). The higher this figure, the looser, and potentially more profitable, the table will be. In our example, we have highlighted a table where the percentage is 71. Play the correct strategy here, and with an average run of the cards you should do well.

However, having joined a loose table, don't forget to check the Plrs/Flop percentage from time to time. As the original players leave and are replaced by new ones, this will change and the table may become a tight one. This will be the time to make an exit with your profits and seek out greener pastures.

Relative Table Position

It's a big advantage to have tight players on your immediate right because these players will only raise when they hold a top hand. Because you act after them, you have the opportunity to fold a marginal hand that you might otherwise have bet on.

The choice of where to position yourself at the table is not as important as the selection of the table itself, but still shouldn't be overlooked. You are said to have position on your opponents if they are seated on your right – you act after they do. Therefore, you want your stronger opponents on your right. Usually, this means tight players – those that are very choosy about which hands they choose to play.

With regard to loose players, you want to try to get any maniacs (those that love to bet with very little to back it up) on your immediate left. This presents you with several advantages:

Note that there is some disagreement on this issue. Many people think that you should have tight players on your left as they are more predictable, and loose players on your right as you can fold marginal hands when they raise. This is a matter of opinion, though, as there are pros and cons with either arrangement.

1) You will be able to see how every other player after the maniac reacts to his or her betting.

2) You'll be able to use the maniac as an unwitting partner to knock out the players after him or her. If, for example, you hit a top pair and bet, the maniac may well raise, making it too costly for the others to chase their straight and flush draws.

3) A maniac enables you to be deceptive. Let's say you hit a four-of-a-kind. You check (which suggests you have a weak hand) to the maniac who bets. Everyone knows the maniac has probably got nothing and will call if they have a half-decent hand. When the betting gets round to you again, you can now raise with plenty of money already in the pot.

Identifying Dangerous Opponents

Basically, there are two types of players who are dangerous. The first, not surprisingly, is the poker professional who plays to a strategy, works out the opposition, knows the percentages, and has the courage to make it all stick. This type of player can be hard to spot because they also know how to mix up their play. In general, though, the top-notch poker player plays a tight/aggressive game. This means usually playing only the top start cards but then playing them extremely aggressively. So when you are watching a table to see if it's suitable, and you see a player who folds most of the time but raises persistently when he or she does play, think twice about joining the table. If you do, avoid any confrontations with that player unless you are holding a very good hand indeed.

The second type is the maniac and they are very easy to spot. These people play literally every hand and will often raise and re-raise right down to the river. Most of the time they lose, but now and again (and this is why they're dangerous) they get lucky. The problem with them is that it's impossible to have any idea of what they have. Usually it's nothing, but because they can't be intimidated by a raise, it's impossible to prevent them playing speculative hands. You can have them beaten as far as the final card, but if they get lucky and the right card falls for them, all of a sudden their second-best hand becomes a winning one. The following is a typical example:

Your start cards are an ace and a king. The maniac has the six and three of diamonds. The flop cards are the queen of diamonds, jack of spades and ten of hearts. You therefore have an A-K-Q-J-T straight, while the maniac has nothing other than an outside chance of a diamond flush. With such a good hand you raise and at this point any sensible player would fold.

However, the maniac is not called a maniac for nothing. He or she calls your raise, and the turn card is another diamond. You raise again, and again the maniac calls. The final card is yet another diamond and you're beaten by a flush. You've had the best hand virtually all the way, you've played it correctly, and against any other type of player you would have won. While you should be able to get your money back from the maniac in subsequent hands, you need to be wary with this kind of player.

Many good players visit the lower limit tables occasionally to rebuild their bankroll after a run of bad luck. As we explain here, these players can usually be recognized by the way they play.

When the cards are falling for them, maniacs can make a big dent in your chip stack. This is when you will need an adequate stack and the ability to keep calm. If you have both, in the long term you will usually get all your money back, plus some.

Identifying Weak Opponents

Commonly known as "fish" in poker parlance, weak players are what any good player is looking for. Finding a table swimming with them is a dream come true. Look for the following:

Make a note of any weak players you come across in the poker room's Buddy List. Most players tend to stick to the same poker room, and so you will often be able to find them in subsequent sessions. If you make a habit of doing this, you will soon have a good list of players that you are able to beat.

- Players who play too many hands. While we have already mentioned this, it bears repeating. Players who do this just cannot win – it's statistically impossible

- Maniacs who persist in playing to the river in the hope of catching a lucky card. Finding one of these is the poker equivalent of stumbling across a gold mine. Just bear in mind that you can come unstuck against maniacs occasionally, as we explained on the previous page

- Players who give themselves a boastful sounding alias. This is usually a sign of immaturity, and immature people are usually bad poker players

- Players who are losing consistently. They may not be genuine fish, but just down on their luck. In either case, you should take advantage

Number of Opponents

Quite simply, the more opponents you have, the less chance you have of winning any one hand. In all poker rooms the majority of the tables are ten-seaters, with a limited number of six-seaters, and maybe one or two two-seaters (known as heads-up).

In general, we do not recommend that beginners play at six-seat tables. The action is a lot faster and this tends to attract the better players. By all means give it a try in an effort to shake your game up but don't make a habit of it. Short-handed play (which is what this is) requires a different strategy.

Because there are so many opponents to beat, playing ten-seaters can require a lot of patience and self-discipline, particularly if the cards aren't falling for you. If you find yourself losing patience with constant folding, rather than make a silly move as a result, consider moving to a six-seat table. With four fewer opponents, you will be able to play a greater range of start cards. While you may still not win, playing a few hands will at least stop you getting bored and impatient.

Texas Hold'em – The Basics

This chapter explains the rules of this game, hand rankings, and the relative value of the various hands.

You will learn about hand elements, such as overcards and kickers, what a drawing hand is, and what is meant by terms such as inside straight and flush draws.

Being able to read your opponents is an important part of playing poker and we show you how to do this by gaining clues from the way they react at the table.

Covers

Chapter Four

How to Play Texas Hold'em

Texas Hold'em is the most popular of the online poker games, the extensive television coverage it has received probably being the main reason. Another is the fact that it is one of the easier variations of poker to learn and can be picked up in a few minutes by anyone. A few hours of practice is all that's needed to be able to play with a reasonable level of competence.

Rules of Texas Hold'em

Note that the blinds count towards the first bets of the players who posted them. For example: if you posted a small blind of $2 at a $5/10 table, the other players have to bet at least $5. On your first bet, however, you only have to bet $3 as you have already bet $2. From then on, you have to bet the same minimum amount as the others.

At the beginning of each hand, the two players to the left of the dealer button each place a predetermined stake into the pot. These two stakes are known as the *blinds* (see top margin note), and the act of placing them is known as *posting the blinds*. The player immediately to the left of the dealer posts the *small blind* and the next player on the left posts the *big blind*. The small blind is set at half (rounded down to the nearest dollar) of the table's lower limit, e.g. at a $5/10 table, it will be $2. The big blind is set at the lower limit and so will be $5.

The dealer button passes to each player in turn. The player to the left of the big blind (third from the dealer button) is the first to make a move when the betting starts.

1 Big blind	**2** Small blind	**3** Dealer button

Once the blinds have been posted, two cards are dealt face-down to the players. Each player will be able to see their own cards (the jack and the five in the example above) but not those of their opponents. These cards are known as the start, or pocket, cards.

The player who opens a betting round determines whether the check option (see page 32) will be available to the other players. If this player does check then the next player can also check and so on. However, if a player bets instead of checking, the check option will not be available to the players who follow.

In the first two rounds of betting, all bets are at the table's lower limit, or multiples of it. For example, in the first round at a $5/10 table, if Player A bets, he/she has to stake $5. If Player B calls, he/she has to stake $5. If Player C raises, he/she has to stake $10. If Player D calls, he/she has to stake $10. If Player E re-raises, he/she has to stake $20.

The same applies to the last two betting rounds, except stakes are at the table's higher limit, or multiples of it.

The first round of betting now commences: this stage of the game is known as the *pre-flop*. The first player to bet is the one immediately to the left of the two players who posted the blinds. The amount of money that can be bet depends on whether the game is a fixed-limit, pot-limit, or no-limit game (see pages 36-37). As with all forms of poker, players have options to fold, check, call, or raise.

When the round of betting has finished, the dealer deals three cards face-up in the middle of the table where they can be seen by all the players (shown on the next page). This procedure is known as *dealing the flop*, and the three flop cards are used by each player to make the best hand in conjunction with their start cards.

While there are still two more cards to come, at this stage of the game players will have a good idea of the potential strength of their hand, and whether it's worth persevering with it. Note that a common mistake made by inexperienced players at this point is continuing with hands that have little realistic prospect of winning. Once in a while they will get lucky and hit a good card on the turn or river (see pages 46-47) but, more often than not, they won't and will lose. Judging which hands have a good chance of winning is a basic and very important part of playing poker.

The flop cards

Pre-flop, the two blinds players are the last to act in the betting. However, on all subsequent betting rounds, they are the first to act.

A second round of betting now takes place, starting with the player to the left of the dealer (the small blind). When the round of betting has finished, the dealer deals a fourth face-up communal card. This is known as the *turn* card.

The turn card

The turn card is the fourth community card to be dealt. By this stage you usually need to have a good hand to justify continuing (see page 98).

Starting with the player to the left of the dealer button, another round of betting begins. At the end of this, a final community card is dealt, making a total of five. This is called *dealing the river*.

Assuming you are still in the game, you now have the five community cards and your two start cards with which to make a hand. Typically, by this stage most of the players will have folded. The players remaining will have either hit their hand, or missed it, and thus may be contemplating bluffing their way out of trouble.

The river card

You may fold your cards at any stage in the game if you don't think they are good enough.

A final round of betting takes place, after which all the players remaining in the game reveal their hands. This begins with the player to the left of the last player to call and is known as the showdown. The player with the best hand wins the pot, minus the poker room's rake.

The next game now starts with the dealer button advancing one place to the left. The player who posted the big blind in the previous game now has to post the small blind. The big blind passes to the next player on the left. In this way all the players are obliged to place money in the pot every few hands.

Poker Hand Rankings

Having learned the rules of Texas Hold'em, the next thing you need to know is the range of hands that can be made. The following table lists them in order of ranking.

It is essential that you memorize these hands: online poker is very quick (you have literally a few seconds to make your decision). When you are sitting there with a straight and the flop indicates that another player might have a flush, not knowing which of the two is the best hand can cost you a lot of money.

Royal Flush	Ace, king, queen, jack, and ten, all of the same suit. This is the best hand possible – in the unlikely event of you ever getting one, pray somebody else also has a good hand and bets into you
Straight Flush	Five cards of consecutive rank, all of the same suit. It's very rare to see one of these
Four-of-a-Kind (known as quads)	Four cards of any one rank, and any other card. This hand pops up occasionally and is almost a guaranteed winner
Full House	Three cards of one rank, and two cards of a another rank. An excellent hand with which you'd be very unlucky to lose. (It does happen occasionally, though)
Flush	Any five cards of the same suit. A very strong hand that will usually win
Straight	Five cards of consecutive rank. A strong hand that usually wins
Three-of-a-Kind (known as a set, or trips)	Three cards of the same rank and two unrelated cards. A good hand but often beaten by a straight, flush or full house
Two Pairs	Two cards of one rank, two cards of another rank, and an unrelated fifth card. A reasonable hand that wins many pots
Pair	Two cards of the same rank, and three other unrelated cards. A weak hand that loses more often than not
High Card	Five unrelated cards – no pair, no flush, no straight – nothing. Not considered as a hand

Whichever version of poker you play, the hands in the table above are the ones you will be trying to make. In some games, such as Omaha Hi/Lo, Seven-Card Stud Hi/Lo, and Razz, there is another type of hand known as a low-hand in which players are trying to hit five cards below a nine. (We'll see more on this later.)

Poker Hand Values

Now that you know the poker hands, we'll show you their relative values.

A pair of aces is the best starting hand you can get. Perversely, however, it can also be the worst if you don't know when to fold it. Many players get trapped by this hand because they play it to the end. Unfortunately, if all you've got at the final stage of the game is a pair, you are more likely than not to lose.

Pairs

A pair is the most common hand in poker. High pairs – A-A, K-K, Q-Q, and J-J – win many games; middle and low pairs usually lose.

In general, pairs are dangerous hands (for you) and they are often over-played by beginners. Many players place too much reliance on top pairs, thinking the game is as good as won, and persist with middle and low pairs in the hope of making a set (a three-of-a-kind). In the case of top pairs, they forget that these are still the lowest type of hand and are easily beaten.

Low and middle pairs rarely win pots. These hands almost always need to be improved to stand a chance of winning.

Over-playing pairs is particularly dangerous in low-limit Hold'em, where many players routinely draw to the river in the hope of making a set. The more players there are staying in the game to the end, the more likely it is that a pair will be beaten. As you move up the limits, however, where the stakes are higher, players are naturally more cautious with the result that pairs have more value.

Note that, statistically, a pair of aces will win approximately one game in three. A pair of twos, on the other hand, will win only one game in twelve.

Two Pairs

Many large pots are won with these hands, especially if one of the pairs is A-A or K-K. A two-pair hand can be particularly lethal if neither pair is on the board. (Such a pair is known as a split pair.) For example:

A hand containing two pairs is much more powerful than one containing a single pair. These hands can be played with more confidence.

Flop Cards

Turn Card

River Card

Let's say Tom is holding A-A; he's going to love these community cards.

A flush is a five card hand as it requires five cards of the same suit. Because you have only two start cards, a flush is only possible when there are three cards of the same suit on the table.

He has the highest pair, there's no chance of being beaten by a flush (see top margin note), a straight is very unlikely, and there's a king, which, hopefully, another player has paired with and will bet on. There's no apparent danger to his aces.

However, Jane is holding K-9 in her start cards giving her two (split) pairs. Unfortunately, Tom has no way of deducing this from the cards on the board. The first clue he is going to get will be on the river when Jane stays in the betting. By this time, though, the damage will be done. Even if Tom folds his aces then, he'll still have lost a large pot.

Playing a two-pair if one of them is on the board requires more caution, as there is a chance that someone has a third card of that rank, making a set.

Sets (Three-of-a-Kind)

When we say "the board" we are referring to the community cards in the middle of the table.

Also known as "trips", this is another hand that can catch players by surprise. If only one of the three cards is on the board (a concealed set), opponents have no indication that they are up against one.

If you are dealt a pair, you have a 1 in 7.5 chance of hitting a set on the flop.

Players holding sets will usually win the game as they beat the most common hands, pairs and two-pairs. However, you need to be aware of the possibility of another player holding a straight, or a flush.

Straights

An inside straight is where the hand is completed by an inside card. For example: 4-5-7-8 needs a 6.

An outside straight needs an outside card. For example: T-J-Q-K is completed by a 9 or an A. Because two cards can complete the hand, the chances of completing an outside straight are much higher.

If you get one of these you can be fairly confident that you are going to win the game. The only hand that's likely to beat you is a higher straight, or a flush.

These hands can be either low-ended or high-ended. For example, a low-ended straight would be when you hold 7-8 and the board (see middle margin note) is 9-10-J. If you hold K-Q with the same board then you have a high-end straight.

You can also have a situation where the straight can be completed only from one end, e.g. A-2-3-4 needs a 5 (a one-ended straight).

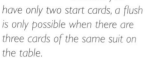

The problem with straights is that it's often fairly obvious from the board cards, and the way he or she is betting, when a player is holding one. Because of this, often a straight will only win a smallish pot as the other players have seen the danger and folded.

Although they are lesser hands, split pairs and concealed sets are more likely to win a large pot as opponents have no way of seeing them coming.

Flushes

A flush is an excellent hand to hold and it is unlikely to be beaten. Because of this, most players will draw to the river if there is a chance of hitting one. However, in most cases this is a mistake. We'll look at this in more detail later on, but for now let's see what the statistics tell us.

Being dealt two suited cards is common – you can expect this once in every four games.

If you have a three-flush (two more cards of the same suit needed) after the flop, the probability of hitting two more suits on the turn and the river is 1 in 23. Thus, the chances of completing your flush are slim, and a huge pot will be needed to justify playing the hand out (see Playing the Percentages on pages 62-65).

If you have a four-flush after the flop (one more card needed), the probability of making the flush on the turn or river is 1 in 2, which is much better odds. However, if the turn card doesn't complete the flush, the odds of making it on the river card go up to 1 in 4.

The most important statistic of all is that two suited start cards will make a flush once in every 16 attempts. This indicates quite clearly just what a futile exercise chasing after flushes really is. Furthermore, if you play low-suited cards, there is also the danger that even if you hit the flush, a higher one will beat you anyway.

Many players lose a lot of money by chasing after flushes (and straights). When they do finally get one, the pot is rarely large enough to cover the losses incurred on the previous attempts, never mind show a profit.

Throughout this book, you will see many references to straight and flush draws. This refers to a hand with which a player is hoping to make either a straight or a flush.

Remember this statistic: the odds of hitting a flush from two suited start cards are 1 in 16.

Full Houses

Hit one of these and your face will split open in a wide grin. You won't be able to get your money in the pot fast enough. However, you need to be aware that a full house can be made in two ways, and if it falls the wrong way, you could actually have a terrible hand.

Whenever you get a full house where three of the cards are on the board, be extremely wary. Effectively, all you have is a pair and the hand should be played on that basis.

This is due to the fact that a full house is essentially two hands – a pair and a set. If the set is on the board then everybody else has it as well. So if two players are also holding a pair (which is very common) then both will have a full house. It then becomes a game of pairs, and the player with the highest pair will win (and there's also the possibility that someone might have the fourth card of the set's rank to give them quads – see below).

For the player with the lower pair, this is a truly horrible hand to get as he or she will have put a load of money in the pot before waking up to the reality of the situation.

The thrill of hitting a full house is rare, and often blinds a player to the possibility that another player might have a higher one, or quads. This is by no means an uncommon scenario.

How to play an unbeatable hand is a skill in itself, and is something you will need to know how to do. We look at this on page 68.

Quads (Four-of-a-Kind)

Hitting four cards of the same rank is very unusual. The possibility that someone has higher quads is always there but, in reality, is so unlikely that you can discount it completely.

The only problem you will have is how to play the hand so as to extract the maximum amount of money from your opponents.

Straight Flushes

A straight flush is the ultimate poker hand, be it a royal flush or otherwise. Quite simply, if you get one of these, you are virtually unbeatable. The chances of getting one, though, are very remote.

As with quads, the only decision you will face is how to play the hand in order to get the most out of it.

Hand Elements

If you hit a good hand never discount the possibility that someone else has hit the same hand. Remember that five cards are shared, so this happens frequently. For this reason, it's important to have a high kicker.

Two elements of a poker hand that are commonly overlooked by beginners are kickers and overcards. Understanding what these are, and their relevance in a game of poker, is essential.

Kickers

Kickers are the left-over cards after a hand is declared, and are the determining factor in who wins if two or more players have the same hand. Kickers are only relevant in hands that don't require five cards, i.e. sets, two-pairs, one-pair, and high card situations. Here is an example:

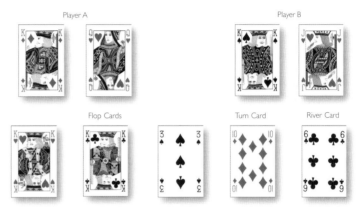

Here, both players have a set (three kings). However, Player A has a queen kicker while Player B has a jack kicker. Thus, Player A takes the pot.

Kickers are particularly relevant in situations where you are attempting to win the game with a pair. At a ten-seat table, it is not unusual for two players to be holding the same pair, usually the higher ones, such as kings, queens, and jacks. The higher the kicker, the higher the chance of the pair winning.

Another common situation is where there is a set on the board. The player with the highest kicker (assuming it's higher than the left-over cards on the board) will win. If none of the players has a kicker higher than the left-over cards then the pot is split.

Overcards

An overcard can be defined in two ways:

1) It is a start card that is higher than any card on the board. For example, if you hold A-K and the board is Q-8-5, you have two overcards, as shown below.

Start Cards   Flop Cards

If there are overcards (particularly if they are high ones, such as aces or kings) on the board, look at them as a beware sign. If you fail to make at least a pair higher than the highest overcard, you will usually lose the hand.

2) It is a card on the board that is higher than either of your start cards. For example, if you hold T-5 and the board is 2-4-A, there is an overcard (the ace) on the board, as shown below.

Start Cards Flop Cards

There will be many occasions when all you hold on the flop are two overcards, as shown in example 1 above. As a general rule, in this situation you should fold because if you play, the best hand you are likely to make is just a pair. Unfortunately, a pair (even a top pair) is not going to win enough hands to justify the expense of putting double bets in the pot on the turn and river stages. The times you hit your pair and win will not make up for the times you hit it and lose.

If you are new to Texas Hold'em, you will do better by folding all overcard hands. Until you know how, and when, to play them, these hands will be money losers.

Beginners are advised not to play overcards at all. If they do, they will almost certainly lose as a result. More advanced players do play overcards successfully but the conditions need to be correct to do this.

See page 96 for more details on this subject.

Drawing Hands

Over-playing drawing hands will result in a slow, but steady, erosion of your bankroll.

A drawing hand is one that needs to be improved. For example, 5-6 is a drawing hand because the chances of winning with a 6 high are virtually nil. A pair of kings, on the other hand, is a made hand and will win many pots with no improvement.

The three most common drawing hands players try to make are sets, straights, and flushes. When they do hit them, they will usually win the pot. However, you need to be aware of two things here:

1) For every time you hit the hand, there will be many more when you don't (and almost always lose money). This takes us on to the second point.

2) When you do hit the hand, the pot must be big enough to cover the odds against hitting it (see pot odds on pages 63-64).

The majority of hands are drawing hands, so playing them all is a sure-fire way to lose your bankroll. To win with these hands, there are three factors you must consider:

The whole purpose of playing poker is to win money. If it's costing you $10 to win $8 then you are losing money. If you are playing a drawing hand, you must be sure that, if you win with it, the size of the pot warrants the risk.

● Which hands to play
● Whether the size of the pot is going to make the play worthwhile
● At what point to give up on the hand

Something else to remember is that straights and flushes require at least three of the hand's cards to be on the board. This often makes it fairly obvious to your opponents what they might be facing. For example, if three cards of a straight are on the board, e.g. 5-6-7, and the turn card is an 8, this is going to kill the game – anyone who doesn't hold a 4 or a 9 will fold immediately if an opponent bets.

For this reason, pots won with these hands are often quite small. To win a large pot usually requires the hand to be completed on the turn or river, by which stage money has already gone into the pot.

We'll take a much closer look at this in Chapter 6.

The Importance of Table Position

A player's position at the table in relation to the dealer is an extremely important strategic factor in Texas Hold'em, and one that is totally ignored by most online players. Table position is a major factor when deciding which start cards should be played and which should be folded. For example, a top hand can be played in any position, while a lesser hand should be played only in a late position where an informed decision can be made based on previous players' actions.

Early Position

The four players sitting to the left of the dealer, including the two blinds, are in early positions. Because they have to act first in the betting, they are at a disadvantage as they cannot observe how their opponents will act before making their move.

For example, in an early position you could bet on a marginal hand and may then find yourself faced with a raise by a later player, making it more expensive to play on with that hand. If you'd been in a late position, however, the raise would have come before it was your turn to act, and so instead of betting on the marginal hand, you could have folded and saved yourself a bet.

This is why it's so important to play only the top start cards in early position. If another player does raise you, it doesn't matter because you're going to play these cards anyway. In fact, you don't mind being raised because at this point in the game you will usually have the best hand.

Middle Position

The three players to the left of the early position players are said to be in a middle position.

Pre-flop, these players don't have the benefits of late position, but neither do they have the disadvantage of being in an early position. Because they are between the two, they are able to play a few more hands than they would in an early position, but not as many as they could in a late position.

After the flop, they have the benefit of having seen half their opponents act, but are handicapped by the fact that they don't know what the other half are going to do.

When in an early position, players need to be very selective about which hands they play. If they bet on a weak hand and then someone after them raises, the correct play is to fold. This will cost them their bet, though. By playing only top hands in this position, they will have no reason to fold to a raise.

A very important thing to remember about table position is that you will be in the same position for every betting round in any one hand. (The only exception to this is the blind players who are last to act in the first betting round, but first to act in every subsequent round.)

Late Position

The final three players are in late position. This is the best position on the table as it provides many advantages, the most important of which is that they have a lot of information available to them.

Being one of the last to act gives you two crucial pieces of data: a) how many opponents you are playing against, and b) their actions.

In the example here, Td means the ten of diamonds and 5d means the 5 of diamonds. This convention will be followed throughout the book, with s to indicate spades, c for clubs and h for hearts.

Let's assume you have Td-5d. This is a drawing hand and with these particular cards, you will be hoping to hit a flush. The problem with drawing hands is that the odds against completing them are high. This means you need to win a large pot to make the play profitable, and the only way the pot will be large is if a good number of your opponents are making bets.

Being the last to act, you will know exactly how many players have made a bet. If seven players fold and only two bet, you would fold your Td-5d. But if seven bet and only two fold then you would play the hand. In an early position, you would have folded immediately as you wouldn't have had the opportunity to see how many players made a bet.

Late position allows a player to take a chance with lesser hands. These are hands you would fold in an earlier position for fear of a raise behind you.

A low to middle pair is another example of a hand that can only be played in a late position, and with this you would be looking to hit a set. However, you wouldn't want to put too much money on these cards, and would only play them if you could see the flop cheaply. Being last to act tells you this as well: if no one has raised, you can see the flop for one bet, which makes the play worthwhile. If someone has raised, however, you will have to pay two bets; also, their raise indicates they have a good hand. So you would fold.

Other advantages include:

- Being able to buy a free card (see page 67)
- The opportunity to "steal" the blind money (see page 79)
- Opportunities to bluff (see pages 69-70)
- Being able to "buy" a better table position (see page 67)

We'll look at these in more detail later on.

Playing Styles

A big part of playing poker is avoiding predictable play. This is a trap that many players fall into. If you always play the same way, other players will soon notice and take advantage. For example, if you rarely call a raise, you will find yourself being bluffed out of many pots. Mix your play up a bit to keep your opponents guessing.

While using the right strategy and playing the percentages will give you a big edge over the vast majority of players, there are other ways to increase your edge over them further. One of these is being able to recognize the different playing styles adopted by players, most of which result in consistent losses. Once you can do this and understand why they lose, you will then have a good idea of what they are thinking and be able to second-guess them.

Loose-Aggressive

Loose-aggressive players are known as maniacs as they play most hands and call most bets. They have no grasp of good poker strategy, no conception of the percentages, and go all in at the drop of a hat. These players rely totally on luck and, in the short term, can be successful. When their luck runs out though, so do their chips. Play this way and you are guaranteed to go broke very quickly indeed.

Loose-Passive

Slightly better than the maniac, the loose-passive player also plays most hands. However, players of this kind rarely raise; instead, they simply call or check every bet regardless of how good their hands may be. As they're never in control of the betting and don't take advantage of good hands, they are destined to be losers – not as quickly as the maniac, but losers nevertheless.

Studying the way in which your opponents play can pay big dividends. For example, if an opponent who usually checks and calls suddenly starts raising and re-raising, you just know he or she is sitting on a really good hand. Conceding to this player may not win you anything but it could well save you a bundle.

Tight-Passive

Known as "rocks", these players take no risks at all. They fold continuously, playing only with the very top hands. However, when they get that elusive top hand, they don't play it aggressively enough. Instead of raising and re-raising, they will usually call and check. The problem with this type of play is that it is very predictable. When these players do raise, everyone knows they have a very good hand and folds immediately. They win only very small pots usually.

Tight-Aggressive

If there is an ideal playing style, this is it. These players play only good start cards but play them aggressively by raising at every opportunity. When they get a good hand, they go for the kill. Bad hands, they fold. This is the best way to win at poker.

Poker Tells

A poker tell is any habit or physical reaction that gives other players information about your hand. For example, some people when holding a really strong set of cards are unable to hide a slight tremor in their hands. Others will glance at them repeatedly as if to reassure themselves that their eyes are not deceiving them. There are many more, and experienced players know them all and act on them.

However, in online poker your opponents are invisible, so is it possible to get any tells? It certainly is. The following can give you a good indication regarding the strength of your opponents' hands.

A Long Delay Followed by a Bet or Raise
Most players who take longer than usual before betting are trying to create the impression that they have a weak hand and are having to think hard about whether it's worth playing, when in reality they actually have a strong hand. They do this to encourage you to bet.

Checking

Players who check at every opportunity usually have a poor hand, and are easily bluffed out of small pots.

Players usually check when they have a weak hand as it enables them to stay in the game at no cost. Players who check at the flop can often be bluffed out of the game by making a bet. They're not prepared to risk calling a bet on a poor hand and, as they have little invested in the game at this early stage anyway, will let it go. You can pick up useful small pots this way.

Instantaneous Bet or Raise on the Turn or River
This is a sign of confidence and usually indicates a very strong hand. Players who do this (especially when raising) are confident that they have the best hand and can't wait to take your money. If someone does this to you, be careful; take a few seconds to re-evaluate the board and see if there's something you've missed.

In the latter stages of a game be careful if a player starts betting instantaneously. This usually means he or she has a very good hand and is confident of winning with it.

Check-Raise
A check-raise is when a player initially checks, and then when the betting comes round again, raises. The check is to make the other players think he or she has a weak hand and thus put money in the pot. This accomplished, the player then starts raising. When you see someone doing this, it is a sure sign that this person has a good hand.

Inside the Mind of a Poker Pro

We're going to try to get inside the head of a top poker player and identify the characteristics that make him so good. Comparing yourself to this hypothetical character will give you a good idea whether or not you have what it takes to play winning poker.

Very few people possess all the mental characteristics necessary to be a top poker player. This is why there are so few of them. If you are reading this book (and probably others) with this intention in mind, be aware that good poker technique will only take you so far.

Purpose

Our man has one thing in mind when he sits down at a poker table: taking the other players' money. He's not there to enjoy himself or to pass the time – this isn't a game to him; it's business.

Focus

He allows nothing to distract him from his purpose. He can't be bullied or intimidated by the other players. When he's playing, he shuts his private life away – personal problems do not affect his play.

Intelligence

He has an analytical brain and is able to do quick mental calculations that enable him to figure out the percentages. He knows which hands to play and how far to play them. He can "work out" his opponents and second-guess them.

Discipline

Our man is able to "shut up shop" when things are going against him. There is no way this guy is going to lose a cent more than he has to. This enables him to ride out losing streaks that would cripple lesser players.

Patience and self-discipline are two of the most important assets a gambler can have. Without these, you are beaten before you start, regardless of how skillfully you play.

Observation

He sees everything. He looks for tables with weak players, he knows all the poker tells, and he recognizes danger signs. He can often tell you what cards you are holding.

Cool

The man is unflappable; nothing fazes him. He doesn't get excited and over-confident when he wins, and he doesn't go "on-tilt" (see page 166) when he loses.

Patience

He doesn't expect to be winning all the time; he knows it isn't possible. He'll just sit and wait for good opportunities.

Poker Ploys

Basic strategy (as described in Chapter Six), will only take you so far in poker. If you want to be a really good player, you will need to have more weapons in your arsenal.

The techniques described in the following pages will take your game to a different level – one that few of your online opponents will ever reach.

Covers

Chapter Five

Playing the Percentages

If you are a percentage player, you are not a gambler. You will be doing exactly the same thing that casinos do: stacking the odds in your favor. If you get it right, it will be impossible for you to lose in the long term. Compare this with the player who doesn't play the percentages: that player is a gambler, and in the long term will find it impossible not to lose.

The vast majority of poker players base their game on luck. They play speculative hands *hoping* to catch the card they need, they play so-called "lucky cards" because they've won with them before, and they attribute their losses to bad luck. Periodically, they do get lucky, but the law of averages says that for every lucky streak they get, they will also have an unlucky one.

Luck is a factor in poker, of course (as it is in any game of chance), but to a good player, it is much less of one; it is a short-term issue, and in the long term it's largely irrelevant. The reason for this is that good players are able to recognize when the odds are in their favor and when they aren't. This knowledge enables them to drop hands that in the long term are going to lose them money. Inexperienced players who don't understand odds will bet on these hands.

As a very simple illustration, consider this: Diamond Jack says to Bill "Let's toss a coin 1000 times. If it comes down heads, you pay me $100 and if it comes down tails, I'll pay you $90". If Bill accepts, he'll win $90 500 times and lose $100 500 times. At the end of the 1000 spins, he'll be $5000 out of pocket. Bill may get lucky periodically and he may find himself up at times, but over 1000 spins the law of averages will take over. This is an impossible game for Bill to win – the odds are stacked against him. Fortunately, Bill's not stupid. There's no way he's going to bet on a game he simply cannot win. He just laughs at the ludicrous suggestion.

By evaluating bets in statistical terms, you make sure you are getting value for money. It's much the same as backing a horse to win at 2/1 rather than at evens. At 2/1, you stand to win twice as much for the same stake, making the bet, potentially, twice as profitable.

"OK then" says Diamond Jack (who's an experienced poker player), "I can see you're not stupid enough to fall for that one. How about 1000 hands of poker". Bill (who's not an experienced poker player) agrees, and after 1000 hands, he's $5000 down. He'll probably never know it but he had no more chance in the poker game than he would have had spinning the coin. While he understands the concept of odds, he had no idea of its importance in a game of poker. Diamond Jack did.

Diamond Jack and Bill are players from opposite ends of the poker spectrum. Bill is the archetypal loser and Diamond Jack is one of the few who win consistently. Let's see how Diamond Jack's knowledge of poker odds helps him to win.

Diamond Jack knows that he's going to lose more hands than he wins – with anything up to ten opponents, it can be no other way. So the only way he can make a consistent profit is to win more with the hands that do win than he loses on the hands that lose. For this to happen, the odds must be stacked in his favor, as they were when tossing the coin. With really good hands this is not so important as he will win with most of these anyway. It's the lesser hands where he has a good chance of losing where it really applies.

To know what odds he is facing on a hand, he needs to consider two factors: the pot odds and the hand odds.

 A quick method of working out approximate hand odds in percentages is as follows:

At the flop – multiply the number of outs by four. For example, if you have a flush draw, there are nine outs; 9 x 4 = 36. So you have roughly a 36 % chance of completing the flush (the exact odds are actually 35 %).

At the turn or river – multiply the outs by two. Using our flush example; 9 x 2 = 18. You have roughly an 18 % chance (the exact odds are 19.6 %).

While they are not exact, the results are accurate enough.

Pot Odds

Pot odds is the relationship between the size of the pot and the size of a bet. For example: if there is $10 in the pot and you have to call a $2 bet to stay in the game, then the pot odds are 5:1. You stand to win $10 for a $2 stake. If you have to call a $5 bet in the same $10 pot then the pot odds are 2:1. Obviously, the higher the pot odds, the more value you are getting for your bet.

Hand Odds

This is the statistical likelihood of making a particular hand. To work it out simply divide the number of cards that won't complete the hand by the number of cards that will (the latter are known as "outs"). For example: your pocket cards are J-T and the flop is Q-3-9. You need an 8 or a K to complete a straight. What are the chances of making it?

Of the 47 unseen cards (52 cards in the pack minus the two start cards and the three flop cards) there are eight cards that will complete the hand (four kings and four eights) and 39 that won't. Simply divide 39 by eight to give a figure of 4.8. Thus, approximately every five times you play this hand, you will complete the straight once; the other four times, you won't.

Using the Percentages

Simply compare the hand odds to the pot odds. If the odds against making your hand are higher than the pot odds, then the potential payoff from winning doesn't justify the bet.

The description of using the pot odds on this page fails to take one factor into account – the possibility of an opponent making another bet after you have worked out the odds. This will increase the pot odds. This factor is known as "implied odds" and is defined as the relationship between the size of the current pot and the size of the final pot.

What this boils down to is that sometimes you can bet on a hand that the pot odds say you shouldn't do because the implied odds will make it correct to do so. For example: the pot holds $200 and you need to bet $20 to call the previous bet. Thus, the pot odds are 10:1. The odds of hitting your hand, however, are 1:11, so you should fold. But, if two opponents each make another bet, the pot goes up to $240 and the pot odds become 12:1. If you have reason to believe they will both make the bet, the implied odds say you will be correct to call.

For example: you are holding 5-6, and the flop shows an 8-9-A. You need a 7 to complete an inside straight. There are four outs for your hand (four 7s in the deck). The odds of making this hand are 1:11.

There is $80 in the pot, and it's $10 to call; this makes the pot odds 8:1. Thus, for the hand to break even it must win once in eight instances. However, the hand odds say it will win once in eleven instances. If you bet on this hand eleven times, you will have staked a total of $110 and won $80 – a net loss of $30.

Another example: your start cards are both spades and the flop brings two more. You need one more spade to make a flush. As there are thirteen spades in the pack and four are already showing, you have nine outs. The odds of making a hand with nine outs are 1:4.

Assuming the betting and the size of the pot are the same as in the example above, the pot odds are 8:1. Again, you need the hand to win once in eight instances to break even. The hand odds say the hand will win once in four instances, so if you bet on it four times, you will have staked $40 and won $80 – a net profit of $40.

All this is dependent on the hand actually winning and, of course, sometimes it won't. To cover this possibility, you need some leeway in the pot odds (they need to be slightly higher). If the odds are good, the leeway's probably there already, but if not, the hand may be too risky to play.

All serious poker players play the percentages and it gives them a definite edge over the players who don't. To do it, though, (particularly online where the pace is fast), requires some quick mental arithmetic that is not so easy to perform in the heat of a game. However, because the other players cannot see you, there is nothing to prevent you from using some aids.

Working out the pot odds is easy with a calculator; it takes only a couple of seconds. As regards hand odds, all you need is the following table, which shows you the odds against making the most common hands in Texas Hold'em.

The Hand column shows common hands, and the Outs column shows the number of outs (cards) that can complete the hand. Taking the first line as an example, if you have a set after the flop, there is only one card, or out, that can give you quads.

The Flop column gives the odds of completing the hand with two cards still to come, the Turn column gives the odds of completing the hand with the turn card, and the River column gives the odds of completing the hand with the river card.

Outs	Hand	Flop	Turn	River
1	Set to quads	1:22.5	1:46	1:45
2	One pair to a set	1:11	1:22.5	1:22
3	One overcard to a pair	1:7	1:14.6	1:14.3
4	Two pairs to a full house Inside straight draw to a straight	1:5	1:10.7	1:10.5
5	One pair with an overcard to a set, or two pairs with the overcard	1:3.9	1:84	1:8.2
6	Two overcards to a pair	1:3.1	1:6.8	1:6.6
7	Set to a full house	1:2.5	1:5.7	1:5.5
8	Outside straight draw to a straight	1:2.1	1:4.8	1:4.7
9	Flush draw to a flush	1:1.8	1:4.2	1:4.1
10	Over-pair with an outside straight draw to a set, or a straight	1:1.6	1:3.7	1:3.6
11	Overcard with an outside straight draw to a pair, or a straight	1:1.4	1:3.2	1:3.1
12	Flush, and inside straight draw to a flush or a straight	1:1.2	1:2.9	1:2.8
13	One pair, and an outside straight draw to two pairs or better	1:1.0	1:2.6	1:2.5
14	Outside straight draw, and two overcards to a straight or a pair	1:09	1:2.3	1:2.2
15	Outside straight flush draw	1:08	1:2.1	1:2.0

Committing the odds in the table opposite to memory, so that they can be recalled instantly, will prove to be very beneficial. If you don't fancy the idea of doing this, though, at least memorize the odds for flush and straight draws. You'll be using these all the time.

Note that hands with fourteen outs, or more, are odds-on to complete. Thus, you can play these hands regardless of the pot odds.

Raising

Until players understand the power of the raise and the various ways it can help them achieve their goal, i.e. win the pot, they're never going to succeed at poker.

Building the Pot

This is the most obvious reason to raise. You're sitting on A-A and the flop is A-A-K. You've hit a monster hand and want to win as much with it as possible. So the natural inclination in this situation is to raise. While this might work, it may, however, have the opposite effect. It could actually intimidate your opponents into folding and result in you completely wasting the hand.

The trick with using the raise to build the pot, therefore, is picking the right time to do it. Using the above example, if you raise on the flop, players who haven't made a hand will usually fold. However, if you call, or maybe even just check, they may stay in for the turn card, which, hopefully, will complete their hand giving them an incentive to bet. Now will be the time to raise. If there are several players still in, you might even leave it until the river before you raise. Remember, the more cards your opponents see, the better the chance they have of making a hand.

The other thing to remember is that bets double on the turn and river, so this is where you'll want to see your opponents betting.

Limiting the Competition

Many players fail to grasp one of the most fundamental concepts in poker – the more opponents you have, the smaller your chances are of winning. Therefore, in most situations, you want as few players in the game as possible as this greatly lowers the odds against you winning the hand. A typical example of this is a pair: J-J, for instance. Play this to the end against nine opponents and it's extremely unlikely to win. If there are only two opponents, though, it stands a much better chance.

So what you do is raise pre-flop. This tells the opposition that you have a good hand and that they'd better beware. Hopefully, they will take the hint and fold. While not all will, especially in a low-limit game where players tend to take more risks, enough will do so to give the hand a much better chance of taking the pot.

As a general rule, raising is much more effective at the higher limit tables. There are two reasons for this:

1) The monetary value of the bet will be much higher, which means that a player who calls it will be risking more.

2) Players at the higher limits are more aware of poker strategy, and thus will be more likely to respect a raise.

Gaining Information

The raise provides a way of finding out the strength of an opponent's hand (albeit at a price). For example: your pocket cards are 9-T and the flop is K-3-T, giving you T-T – a good hand but nothing wonderful. There are two players still in, and either could be sitting there with K-K. A raise at this point is likely to achieve one of two things: firstly, both opponents might fold, thus presenting you with an uncontested pot, or secondly, one might re-raise you. With one king already showing, the other player's re-raise tells you quite clearly that he or she probably has two kings, so you fold. OK, it's cost you a bet to find out you're beaten, but it may well have saved you several bets down the line.

Buying a Free Card

Before trying to buy a free card, you need to be sure the following two conditions are met:

1) You need to be in a late position (last to act, ideally).

2) The opposition need to be the type who are likely to check when given the opportunity to do so.

How can a card be free if you have to buy it? Simple, it can't. This is actually a misnomer: a more accurate description is a cheap card. The purpose is to get to see the next but one community card without having to pay a full bet. Typically, this is done at the flop when the betting is still at the lower limit. For this ploy to work, you need to be in a late position and facing limited opposition.

For example: your pocket cards are 9s-8s and the flop is Kd-Qs-6h. This is not a great hand; at the moment you are probably beaten by a pair of kings or queens. It does have limited drawing potential, though – a backdoor flush or straight. Both are long shots and, unless the pot is huge, you would probably fold it. However, if you are the last to act, throwing in a raise might get you a free card on the river. How? By raising, you will probably make your opponents check on the turn card. If they do then you will have the option to check as well and will be able to see the river card for "free".

Buying Position

You're to the right of the three late position players. You've got a hand that you would play from late position but are wary of playing in your present middle position. If the late position opponents are tight players, throwing in a raise (rather than calling) could well make them all fold. If they do, you've just bought late position, a position you'll hold for every subsequent betting round.

Check-Raising

Before trying a check-raise, be sure that you have an opponent who will make a bet rather than check. You need at least one player to do this, otherwise you won't get the option to raise. Plus, you will actually have made things worse for yourself by giving them a free card, not to mention losing any bets they may have made if you had called.

A check-raise is when you check initially on a betting round and then, when the betting comes back round, you raise.

It is most commonly used when you have a hand that you think is currently the best one but that could be beaten: a set for example. In this situation, you need to knock out some of the opposition to lessen the chances of your hand being beaten, typically by a straight or a flush.

However, if there is a good-sized pot, opponents with drawing hands are going to bet because the pot odds will be in their favor. The only way you are going to persuade them to fold is by reducing the pot odds so that it becomes incorrect for them to bet.

The "nuts" is a term used to describe a hand that cannot be beaten.

This is where the check-raise comes into play. Instead of betting, which will further increase the size of the pot, and thus the pot odds, you check. Opponents with drawing hands will also check because it may give them a free card. However, an opponent with a made hand, such as a high pair, will bet. When the betting comes round to you again, this time you raise. Players with drawing hands will now have to call two bets, which means that the pot odds will be effectively halved, thus making it incorrect for them to call. Therefore, they will fold and you will have achieved your objective of reducing the competition.

However, it is all dependent on an opponent betting. If no one does, you won't have the option to raise (see top margin note).

Slow-Playing

You should never slow-play a hand unless you are certain that it cannot be beaten. While many players do (typically, with sets and straights) and often get away with it, equally often they don't. Usually, they are beaten by the river card, and end up trapping themselves with the second-best hand.

A hand is usually slow-played when it is the nuts (see middle margin note), or very close to it, with the intention of keeping as many players in the game as possible. This is to give them every opportunity to hit their hand; hopefully, a good one that will encourage them to put money in the pot.

To do this, the player with the nut hand checks or calls, rather than raising, so as not to scare anyone off. It's only on the turn, or even the river, that this player makes his or her move by raising (this is when the bets double). By this time, any player who's going to make a good hand will have done so.

Bluffing

When considering a bluff, it is very important that you pick the right type of opponent. Generally, these will be careful or timid players. Also, don't try and bluff more than two: it rarely works.

As with slow-playing, bluffing is an act of deception – but with the opposite intention. Here, you are trying to convince an opponent that you have a better hand than is actually the case.

Bluffing is an important element of poker strategy, and against the right kind of opponent, and in the right type of game, it can be extremely effective. However, in very loose games, such as those commonly found at the low- and micro-limit tables, it is much less so.

Firstly, loose players tend to bite at anything as by their very nature they cannot be intimidated. At the higher-limit tables, however, where players are more circumspect, a bluff is far more likely to be respected. Secondly, if a player doesn't need to put much in the pot to call a bet, as is the case in fixed-limit games, a bluff loses much of its power. In a no-limit game, though, where bets can be huge, it is a fearsome weapon (see page 109).

So when is it appropriate to try a bluff? The following are some typical situations.

When Your Opponents are Tight Players

At fixed-limit tables, bluffing is usually a pointless exercise that is more likely to lose money than it is to win it. You simply cannot make a big enough bet for it to carry any weight.

Tight players are careful players. There are two situations where they can often be bluffed. The first is at the pre-flop stage. Note that for this to be effective, you need to be in late position (last to act, ideally). With a table full of tight players, it is not uncommon for most of them to fold or check, and just one or two to call. Throwing in a raise from last position will often make these players fold.

The second is after the flop. A tight player who's missed the flop will either fold or, if the chance arises, check, in the hope of getting a free card. If you are in late position and two or three opponents all check, by raising you are forcing them to call a double bet to stay in the game, and usually they will fold – presenting you with an uncontested pot.

On the River

Often, players paying to see the river card will be on a drawing hand and will have failed to make it. In this situation, most players will usually check if the option is available.

As anyone with a good hand is going to be betting on the final round, rather than checking, this is a good time to try a bluff.

When there is a Low or Middle Pair on the Board

As with most bluffs, this is more likely to work at higher limit tables where most players will play only high cards. For example, if the flop is 4-4-6, there is a good chance that it has missed everybody. If you raise, the opposition will put you on a set, or a straight, and if they don't have either themselves, will usually fold.

Whenever you try a bluff, though, and someone calls it, you are in a predicament of your own making. To lessen the predicament, you should usually try a bluff only when you have some kind of a hand – a flush, or a straight draw, for example. With only one opponent to beat, you will still have a reasonable chance of winning the game – in this case, though, you will be relying on luck. Win or lose, however, by playing you will at least hide the fact that you were bluffing in the first place.

When Not to Bluff

Almost as important as knowing when to bluff, is knowing when not to. As a general rule, don't try and bluff several opponents. Pre-flop, when they don't have any money in the pot, this may work as they aren't losing anything by folding. After the flop though, it's a different matter.

As soon as you get caught bluffing, the other players will label you as a bluffer, and will be more inclined to call your bets in future. Tighten up your game until they've had time to forget about it.

Never bluff against bad players – it rarely works. Bad players are likely to call anything and everything, a fact that renders a bluff against them utterly pointless. Also, don't bluff if you are in an early table position. You need to see your opponents' actions first.

The opponent is probably the most important factor. Aggressive players who hate to "yield", and maniacs who can't resist betting, should not be bluffed. Weak, timid players, on the other hand, can be.

Deception

Poker is as much about playing the opposition as it is about playing the cards. You should always be watching what your opponents do. Also, don't forget that they will be watching you, so give them something to think about by doing different things occasionally.

The ability to deceive opponents is a very important factor in poker. If you can persuade them that you have a much poorer hand than is actually the case, you are going to take money from them – slow-playing is an example of how you do this. Sometimes, you want to do the opposite and make them think you have a much better hand than theirs: this is bluffing.

If you never try to deceive the opposition then you become a predictable player – one who is going to find it difficult to win. You must be able to mix up your play on occasion, so that your opponents are never quite sure of what you're up to. We've mentioned ways to do this above; here are some others.

Deliberately Play Bad Hands

On page 74, you will see that you should play only certain hands pre-flop. However, if you stick to this religiously, it won't be long before your opponents put you down as a very tight player who must be respected whenever you raise the pot. While you will still win pots, generally they are going to be small ones as opponents aren't going to take any risks with you. Hands that they would play against a loose player, they will fold. When you turn up A-A, raise, and then the entire table folds, you are going to be extremely exasperated.

In your attempts to vary your play, don't be tempted to slow-play high pairs pre-flop. These are your best opportunity of winning and must always be played aggressively by raising. Instead, occasionally play a bad hand (and be seen doing it). This way your opponents won't automatically assume you have a top pair when you raise pre-flop.

So now and again, do the opposite. Wait until you've got a really bad hand, say 6-2, and the flop is completely against you – K-J-T, for example; only an idiot would bet on cards like these. Take this right to the showdown so that the other players will see what you have been playing with. This play will stick in their minds far longer than your good plays. While you will lose money when you do this, the pay-off will come when you get a good hand and your opponents call your bets because they think you may be doing the same thing again.

Switch Gears

Generally, players adopt one of four playing styles (see page 58) and, often, they aren't even aware of it. If you follow the advice in this book, you will be a tight-aggressive player, usually playing only the top hands but playing them aggressively. While this is undoubtedly the best way to play poker, if you *always* play this way, you become predictable.

This is the last thing you want, so, suddenly, become a loose player. You need to pick the right time to do this, though. Remember, loose players lose, and losing isn't in your game plan.

Even if you lose some chips when playing loosely, you will win them back (and more) with your good hands. Opponents will be much more inclined to call your bets when they think you play bad hands.

The ideal time to do it is when the cards are falling in your favor. When you're on a hot streak, you can play virtually anything – even rubbishy hands like 7-2 (the worst possible hand, by the way) will turn into sets and full houses. As soon as your hot streak ends, change back to your normal style.

Your opponents will be totally confused and will be wondering what on earth they're up against. They won't be able to put you down as a bad player, nor will they be able to put you down as a good player. They will have no idea how to play you, and as a result, are much more likely to make mistakes.

Tells

We saw on page 59 how it is possible for players to give definite clues regarding the strength of their hands by the speed with which they make their moves.

In general, try and do the opposite to what most players would do in a similar situation.

Most online players are aware of this, which gives you another way of being deceptive. For example, say you have a four-flush and the river brings an ace of that suit to complete a nut flush. In this situation most players will bet instantaneously knowing they can't lose – you will see this all the time. If you do the same thing yourself, it may well make an opponent pause for thought. So instead, let ten seconds or so go by before making your bet.

Don't make the mistake of waiting until your time to act is almost up. This is another classic indication of a player holding a very good hand. Save this move for when you have missed your hand and want to try and bluff your opponent out of the pot. Combining this with a raise will often do the trick.

Texas Hold'em Strategy

In Chapter Four we showed you the basics of Texas Hold'em, and in Chapter Five you learned some important poker techniques.

In this chapter, we will show you how to put it all together in a strategy that will beat most online players.

Chapter Six

Start Cards

An essential part of mastering Texas Hold'em is knowing which start cards are playable and which are not. The player's position at the table is also a determining factor here.

The table below shows exactly which hands can be played – any hands not in the table should be folded immediately.

Be very selective about which start cards to play – the importance of this cannot be overstated. As a general rule, you should be playing no more than one in five hands. If you are playing more than this, you are playing cards that you shouldn't be.

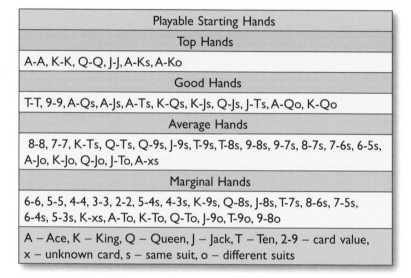

Playable Starting Hands
Top Hands
A-A, K-K, Q-Q, J-J, A-Ks, A-Ko
Good Hands
T-T, 9-9, A-Qs, A-Js, A-Ts, K-Qs, K-Js, Q-Js, J-Ts, A-Qo, K-Qo
Average Hands
8-8, 7-7, K-Ts, Q-Ts, Q-9s, J-9s, T-9s, T-8s, 9-8s, 9-7s, 8-7s, 7-6s, 6-5s, A-Jo, K-Jo, Q-Jo, J-To, A-xs
Marginal Hands
6-6, 5-5, 4-4, 3-3, 2-2, 5-4s, 4-3s, K-9s, Q-8s, J-8s, T-7s, 8-6s, 7-5s, 6-4s, 5-3s, K-xs, A-To, K-To, Q-To, J-9o, T-9o, 9-8o
A – Ace, K – King, Q – Queen, J – Jack, T – Ten, 2-9 – card value, x – unknown card, s – same suit, o – different suits

Playing the start cards listed on this page requires discipline and patience. There will be periods when you fold ten or more successive hands. It will be very tempting to play the odd hand (a pair of eights, for example) just for a bit of excitement. Resist the urge – this is the beginning of a slippery slope.

The hand recommendations are based on a typical middle-limit ten-player game where the action is neither tight nor loose. By playing only these cards, the majority of the time you will have an edge over most of your opponents as you will be playing only the best hands.

Another advantage of this basic strategy is that, to a certain degree, you will be immunized against losing streaks and the mind games these can play with you. If you are only playing a few hands (with this strategy, you will be folding approximately 80% of the time), your losses in a bad streak will be much less.

One negative aspect of playing in this way is boredom. Folding hand after hand can become very tedious after a while. However, watching your bankroll steadily slip away is not very exciting either, and if you don't play this way, that's exactly what will happen.

Pre-Flop Play

Now we'll take a closer look at these hands, explaining in detail how you should play them and why.

Early Positions

These are the four seats to the immediate left of the dealer. Early position players are at a disadvantage as they have to act first, and for this reason they must be very careful in their hand selection.

Playing the Top Hands

With any of these, you raise. If you are re-raised, raise again. Don't hold back: it is essential that you play these hands aggressively. There are two reasons for doing this:

1) To get money in the pot. If two or three players call your raise (or even better, re-raise), money is going into the pot. Remember, at this stage you probably have the best hand.

2) To scare as many of your opponents as possible into folding immediately, thus denying them the chance to draw a better hand on the flop. Your hand rules the roost pre-flop, but afterwards, it might well not do so. The more players who see the flop, the higher the chances are that one of them will hit a flush or straight draw, or a two-pair. If this happens, you will probably lose the hand.

Now you may well be thinking that if you make all your opponents fold, there's going to be nothing in the pot worth winning, and an excellent hand will have been wasted. Remember this, though: at a ten-seat low- or middle-limit table, it's very unlikely that everybody will fold. One or two players will call your raise, which is exactly what you want. Money will go in the pot and, against limited opposition, your top hand has a very good chance of taking it without any improvement. If they do all fold, you still get the blinds money.

What you must not do is slow-play these hands. Many players in this situation will have dollar signs flashing in their eyes, and will be looking to build the pot by keeping as many people in the game as they can. To do this, instead of raising, they call, and even check. The result is nearly always the same. Four or five of their opponents will stay in the game, and at least one of them will end up hitting a better hand.

When you get a top starting hand, get as much money into the pot as possible. You are looking to win with this hand as it stands. The only way to do this is to knock out as much of the opposition pre-flop as you can. Remember, pairs (even big ones) do not fare well against many opponents.

At a ten-seat table, usually four or five players will fold immediately. That leaves you with three or four opponents. If they all bet, three or four bets will go into the pot. However, if you raise and only two of them call, the same amount of money goes into the pot, but you have two fewer players to beat.

Very often, they will make it on the river card. Far from making good use of the top hand, the player will have wasted it completely.

Playing Good Hands

With these cards, you call and wait to see what your opponents do. If someone raises, as a general rule you should then fold. However, before you do, you need to consider the player making the raise (this is where opponent observation pays off). If it was a tight player who plays only top hands, then you should definitely fold. On the other hand, if it was a loose player who rarely folds, then call the bet. If the other player raises you again though, folding is probably the best thing to do (see top margin note).

Playing Average and Marginal Hands

In early position, these hands will only get you into trouble – fold and save your money for a better opportunity.

Middle Positions

Middle positions are the three seats to the left of the early position seats. This is half-way house – you have an idea of the table situation but not the complete picture.

Playing Top Hands

You play these in exactly the same way as you would in early position – raise and re-raise. Top hands don't fall very often – you must make the most of them when they do.

Playing Good Hands

How you play these is dependent on whether you are facing a raise. If not then you can raise with any of these hands. However, if there is a raise after you have played, you should call when the betting gets back to you. If two players make a raise, it's very likely that one of them has you beaten. Do not get into a raising war – just fold.

Playing Average Hands

These hands include many medium ranked connectors. This makes them ideal drawing hands with which to make a flush or a straight. Indeed, hitting one of these is the only way you are likely to win with this type of hand. Their face values are not high, so even if you make a pair, it's unlikely to be the highest pair.

A single raise from a loose player often means nothing. A re-raise, however, indicates that the player has caught a top hand. Unless you also have one, play it safe by folding. Remember, there is no shortage of hands to play. When in doubt, the best policy is usually to leave it.

A connector is two cards of successive rank, e.g. 7-8 or K-Q. If the cards are of the same suit, they are a suited connector. Unless they are of a high face value, in which case they can make a high pair, their value is limited to making a straight or a flush.

The odds against making a flush or straight are high and the attempt to do so is likely to be an expensive one. While you may be very lucky and get the three cards you need on the flop, it's much more likely that you will need the turn card, and probably the river card as well. As the bets double on these rounds, you can see why it is going to be expensive.

Thus, to make this type of play worthwhile, there needs to be a lot of money in the pot. A large pot will usually require four or five players to be contributing, and this is the criterion you use when deciding whether to play a drawing hand. If there are only two or three players still in the game pre-flop then the pot is not going to be large enough. In this case, fold. If you do play, and there is a raise behind you, you should generally fold. Only call a raise if the pot looks like being a huge one.

Marginal Hands

These are mostly low pairs and gapped connectors. Few of them offer a realistic chance of making a good hand (note that you have much less chance of turning a gapped connector into a straight than you do with an ungapped connector). If you bet on these cards from middle position, you run the risk of being raised by a late position player, in which case you would have to fold. The best thing to do with these hands is to dump them straight away.

Late Position

Defined as the last three places at the table, late position gives you many advantages. You've seen your opponents' moves, and thus have a much better idea of which hands are playable and which aren't. Your decisions are easier to make and you have more options regarding the hands you can play.

Playing Top Hands

Raise, raise, raise – there's nothing more to say.

Playing Good Hands

You should play the good hands in exactly the same way as you would in middle position. If someone has already raised, just call the bet. Otherwise, raise and see what the others do. More than likely, most of them will fold. If the remaining players call, throw in another raise to try and narrow the field even more.

You might think that there's as much chance of making a straight with 3-5 as there is with 3-4. There's not. The bigger the gap between the cards, the less chance there is of making the straight.

About the only time you might consider just calling with a top hand is when you are holding Q-Q or J-J, and a very tight player has raised. Players of this type will usually only do this when they are holding A-A or K-K.

Another advantage of being in a late position is that you will be able to calculate the pot odds (see pages 63-64) with a greater degree of accuracy.

Late position also provides an opportunity to "steal" the blinds. If all previous players have checked, throwing in a raise from late position will often make them fold.

Remember, you're not playing top cards now; these hands are vulnerable to high pairs. The fewer opponents you have, the better your chance of winning.

If someone re-raises you then just call. You definitely want to see the flop with these cards but you don't want to pay too high a price.

Playing Average Cards

Flushes, straights, and sets are what you are looking for with these cards. Play them as you would in middle position. Just remember that with these hands you need "value" in terms of the size of the pot to make them worth playing.

If someone raises, you should generally fold. These hands are speculative, so you need to see the flop as cheaply as possible. However, if the pot looks like being a big one, it may be worth calling to see what the flop brings.

Playing Marginal Cards

One of the big advantages of being in a late position is that it allows you to play marginal hands that in any other position you would dump.

Again, the goal with these is flushes, straights, and sets. Low- to middle-card straights can be a particularly effective hand to hold as most players will fold low-card hands. Therefore, the chances of someone else having one are slim. If the flop brings an ace or a king, giving someone a top pair, then a low or middle straight will clean up.

Remember though, these hands are speculative ones and should be played only if you can see the flop without too much expense.

Playing From the Blinds

Some players seem to regard the blind money they have posted as rightfully belonging to them, and thus feel the need to defend it. To this end, they will play cards that they shouldn't, and usually end up losing more as a result. Don't do this yourself. Once the money is in the pot, it's no longer yours.

For the majority of players, playing from the blind positions represents a small but steady drain on their bankroll. There are several reasons for this:

- They are playing "blind". A bet has to be made regardless of the strength of their hand

- They are the first to act in all betting rounds (with the exception of the first one)

- The good players are aware of the disadvantages faced by the blinds players and target them in an attempt to "steal" the blind money

Virtually everything is stacked against them. Unfortunately, most online players either ignore this aspect of their game completely, or over-react to it (see top margin note).

Let's see how you should deal with this situation.

Defending the Blinds

One of the main things the blinds have to contend with is opponents who attempt to steal the blind money. Typically, this will be a late position player who throws in a raise after everyone else has acted, hoping that they will all fold as a result. This player is targeting the blinds money, and assuming that the blinds players have the sense to fold anything other than a top hand.

Blind stealing is much more prevalent at the high limit tables where the monetary value of the blinds bets is much higher. At the micro- and low-limit tables it is much less of an issue and really isn't worth worrying about.

The problem this causes is that if they do fold, the player will try it again – and again – and again. Other players will notice this and, before long, they'll be at it as well. If you allow this situation to develop, your stack will suffer (as will your table image), so something has to be done to stop it.

The solution is to nip it in the bud straight away. The first time someone tries this with you, re-raise them immediately, regardless of what cards you are holding. More than likely, they'll back down and fold. If they do bet, call. Whatever you do, don't fold. Even if you end up losing the hand, you'll have earned their respect and they'll be wary of trying it again (as will the other players).

When you're on the small blind, you need only make half a bet as you've already bet the other half in the blind. Don't regard this as a "cheap" bet and make it regardless of your hand. Instead, see it as an opportunity to save half a bet.

The blinds money is irrelevant here; you're making a statement to the other players – namely, that you're not there to be pushed around.

However, it must be said that at the low-limit tables where the blinds money is a negligible amount, this is not a major issue. Certainly you don't want to allow yourself to be a pushover, but if you try too hard to defend it, you could end up turning a small loss into a big one.

At the high-limit tables, though, it is a completely different matter.

Attacking From the Blinds

By this we mean raising. There are differing opinions as to whether you should raise from the blinds. Ours is that you should do it only with A-A and K-K.

The usual reason to raise pre-flop is when you have a top hand and want to knock out the opposition to increase the chances of it winning. However, by doing this from the blinds (remember, you are last, or next to last, to act), you will be increasing the size of the pot, and thus the pot odds (particularly if you are re-raised by another player).

Far from knocking out the opposition, this will actually give them an incentive to stay in the game because they will now be getting good odds on their drawing hands on the flop. In this situation, your top hand is quite likely to lose, and so your pre-flop raise could well turn out to be an expensive one.

With anything other than A-A and K-K, you will usually be better off calling and seeing what develops on the flop.

Stealing the Blinds

We saw how to do this on the previous page. Is it worth doing, though, considering the trifling sums involved? On low-limit tables, the answer is no. Firstly, the most likely response will be an immediate re-raise putting the onus right back on you. Remember, low-limit players tend to be much more reckless than high-limit players. Secondly, those trifling sums really aren't worth the bother. On high-limit tables, however, where the blind money is much higher, it can be a good tactic against tight players.

Common Pre-Flop Mistakes

Mistakes are how you win money at poker. Not your mistakes though: your opponents' mistakes. It is easy enough to win money when you are getting good hands; the trick is in keeping it. If you avoid making the mistakes listed on this page, you will end up with more money than your opponents because they will lose more than you do.

Poor Start Card Selection

This is the most common mistake of all. Quite simply, if you consistently play hands other than the ones in the table on page 74, you are destined to be a big loser.

Calling When You Should Be Raising

When you hit the top hands, you have your best opportunity of beating the opposition. By calling and checking, you are letting them see cards cheaply. The more cards you allow them to see, the weaker your top hand becomes.

Slow-Playing

Slow-playing to build the pot has its place but not at the pre-flop stage. You only do this after the flop when you have the nuts, or close to it. Doing it pre-flop just gives the opposition the opportunity to stay in the game and make a better hand than yours when the flop cards are dealt.

Not "Listening" to Your Opponents

Every single action taken by your opponents is telling you something. When they raise, it's usually because they have a big hand. When they check, it's usually because they have a weak or marginal hand. If they check-raise, they're often trying to deceive you. If players who usually act quickly take a long time to throw in a raise, they're trying to make you think they have a weak hand. Listen to what they are telling you and act accordingly.

Playing Hands Out of Position

Playing certain types of hand in the wrong position at the table can get you into serious trouble in the later stages of a game.

Not Taking Advantage of Late Table Position

Being the last, or one of the last, to act puts you in a commanding position. You have an opportunity to play hands that are unplayable in any other position, you can make a move on the blinds money, you can get a free community card, and you are in the best position to increase the size of the pot by raising (see bottom margin note).

Most online players fail to take advantage of these benefits.

It is a fact that a player who has once made a bet is more likely to commit to another bet. Being in a late position gives you the ideal opportunity to take advantage of this.

Playing the Flop

The flop is the most important stage in the game. It's at this point that you discover just how good, or potentially good, your hand really is. With the three flop cards and your two start cards, you have 71% of your final hand. The significance of this is that, more often than not, seeing the turn and river cards will not improve your hand further. Usually, the hand you have at the flop is the best hand you are going to make. Realizing this fact will save you many lost bets chasing turn and river cards that don't come.

A common saying is that if the flop fits (improves your hand), bet, and if it doesn't, fold. Generally, this is good advice. Remember, more often than not, drawing the turn and river cards will not improve your hand.

Once you've seen the flop cards, you have many more things to consider than you did pre-flop. These include:

- The strength of your hand, and its potential strength, i.e. the best hand that you are likely to make with it

- The best hand that your opponents are likely to make

- The number of players left in the game

- The players themselves (tight, loose, aggressive, etc)

- Your opponents' actions before the flop

- The pot odds

The first thing to establish is what sort of hand you have and its potential for improvement. Let's see the sort of things you should be looking for with the aid of a sample hand.

Start Cards

Flop Cards

Your start cards are 9d-9c. The flop is Kc-Qs-As. As things stand, your best hand is 9-9. With two more cards to come, realistic possibilities are a two-pair or a set (9-9-9). There is also an outside chance of a 9-T-J-Q-K inside straight.

If your best hand at the flop is a low to middle pair and there are overcards (particularly high ones) on the board, fold the hand. The only exception is if the pot is large enough to warrant trying to hit a set.

Now let's look at these cards from your opponents' perspective. With A-K-Q on the board, someone almost certainly already has a high pair and, quite possibly, two high pairs. There is a good chance that someone will make a T-J-Q-K-A straight, and if anyone is holding two spades, a spade flush is also a strong possibility.

How does your hand stack up against your opponents'? Forget the 9-9, it's beaten already. If you get another 9 to make a set, this increases the possibility of an opponent making a 9-T-J-Q-K straight. If the 9 is a spade then it's quite likely that one of them will also make a spade flush. So while a 9 will improve your hand, it will almost certainly also improve an opponent's hand. Another ace, king or queen would give you two pairs. However, any of these could well give an opponent a set. So whichever way you look at it, this hand is a non-starter.

One of the most important factors in deciding whether to play after the flop is the number of your opponents. The more there are, the better your hand needs to be.

Many of the players you encounter online will play this hand hoping for a third nine, totally oblivious to the fact that if it does come, it will probably complete an even better hand for an opponent.

An important factor when evaluating the flop is the number of opponents still in. The fewer you are facing, the more chance you have of winning with a hand that's not so good. An example would be a middle pair. Against three or four opponents, it stands little chance; against one, or even two, it could hold up.

How your opponents play also needs to be considered. With cautious players who rarely raise, it can be worth trying one more bet to see the next card. If there's an aggressive player behind you though, who's likely to raise, folding will probably save you a bet.

Keep your eyes open for pre-flop raisers who check when the flop brings high cards. They could well have hit a set or a two-pair and be slow-playing to build the pot. A subsequent raise will confirm this.

You should also be aware of what your opponents were doing pre-flop. Someone who was raising probably had a high pair or an A-K. If the flop turns up high cards, they will probably now be on a set, or a two-pair. More raises should have you folding.

With drawing hands, such as straights and flushes, the decision on whether to continue or to fold is based on the pot odds. If the odds are not high enough, persisting with these hands will lose money in the long term.

Playing Pairs on the Flop

Now that you have a good idea of the principles of playing the flop, we'll go into it in more detail with the aid of some specific examples. We'll start with the most common hand – pairs.

The main considerations when playing pairs are overcards and kickers. If the overcards are on the board (against you), then you are at an immediate disadvantage. If you have a low kicker to go with the pair, you are at even more of a disadvantage.

For example:

Start Cards

Flop Cards

Your start cards are Q-Q and the hand was looking good until the flop brought the king overcard. With four or five opponents, you are almost certainly beaten already, and should fold.

Against one or two, though, you may have a chance. In this situation, a raise is a good move. An opponent who does have K-K will probably re-raise you, at which point you fold knowing you're beaten. An opponent who doesn't have K-K will assume that you have it, and will therefore fold.

Calling with a pair at the flop stage is rarely a good move as it achieves nothing: either raise or fold.

Another example:

Start Cards

Flop Cards

You hold Jd-2d and were hoping to see more diamonds on the flop to give you a flush draw. Instead, you've picked up another jack. Still pretty good, you may say.

Playing pairs with a low kicker will get you into trouble time and time again.

Well, that depends on whether you're a gambler or a poker player. If it's the former, this is a good hand to gamble on. With a safe-looking flop, you do have a good chance of winning.

If you're playing poker, though, it's not so clever as there's an equally good chance that you won't win (to win money at poker, you are looking for probabilities, not possibilities).

You may have two jacks, but you also have a low kicker. If four or five players are still in, the chances are high that one of them will also have a jack, but with a higher kicker. This is a classic example of a hand that is shaping up to be the second-best one, and you should fold if there is any serious betting action. Against one or two opponents, you could call and see what develops.

A final example:

Start Cards

Flop Cards

Not knowing when to let go of pairs is a mistake made by far too many players. If the flop doesn't hit them, these are "play and pray" hands.

Here, you have 7-7 with an eight kicker. You have an overcard against you and no chance of a flush or a straight, plus there are two diamonds on the board giving an opponent a possible flush. Your only prospect is hitting another 7 for a set. This hand is junk – dump it.

A slightly different flop, though, makes the hand playable. With two clubs on the board, you need just one more for a flush.

Start Cards

Flop Cards

With two ways of making a good hand (a flush and a set), you now have an excellent drawing hand. If the pot odds are good as well, it's even better. You can call right down to the river with this.

Playing Two Pairs on the Flop

These can fall in one of two ways: boarded, where one of the pairs is on the board and the other is in the player's hand, or split, where one card of each pair is in the player's hand.

The Boarded Two-Pair

Start Cards   Flop Cards

Your start cards are J-J and the flop turns up K-K-5 to give you two pairs. This is a boarded two-pair. There are three likely scenarios here:

1) Everybody has the pair on the board. So any other player who is holding a pocket pair also has a two-pair. If one of them has a pocket pair higher than yours, he or she is in the driving seat.

2) None of your opponents has a pocket pair. Assuming none of them is holding a king either, you are top-dog at the moment.

3) Another player is holding a king and thus has a set (and possibly a five as well for a full house).

So how do you play this hand? Well, the first thing to note is that with two kings already out, there is less chance of an opponent holding another one. Nevertheless, it is still a good possibility and you need to find out now before the bets double.

Therefore, you raise. If you get re-raised, you can assume the re-raiser has a third king. Now, you can fold. If your opponents don't have a king, they are going to think that you have it because you've raised, and will fold themselves. If you get called, you're probably being slow-played and should get out.

Even if you change the cards around to give yourself the two kings and the board the two jacks, the situation is much the same. The danger of an opponent having a set (the jacks), or a full house is still there. Play the hand the same way as above: raise to find out "where you're at".

A two-pair hand where one of the pairs is on the board is no better than a single-pair hand as everybody has the board pair. In fact, it's probably worse because not only do you face the danger of being beaten by someone who has a higher pocket pair, there is also the possibility of someone having a set, or a full house.

The Split Two-Pair

In this scenario, the pairs are split between your start cards and the board, as shown below.

A split two-pair is a much more powerful hand than a boarded two-pair, as the board gives your opponents no clues that you have one.

Start Cards

Flop Cards

A split two-pair is a much stronger hand than a boarded two-pair as there is no pair on the board (this greatly reduces the main threat to a two-pair hand – namely, a set). This hand can be a killer as there's no way an opponent can put you on it.

That said, don't lose sight of the fact that a split pair is still only the second-worst hand. It is beaten by sets, straights, flushes, full houses, and quads. The advice, therefore, is to play it aggressively by raising to make the opposition fold – slow-playing it could cause you a lot of grief at the end. However, if there are still players in at the turn, and the turn card indicates a possible set, flush, or straight for someone, you need to back off. For example:

Don't ever be tempted to slow-play a two-pair hand. While you may well get away with it, there are simply too many ways for it to be beaten. With a two-pair, you should be raising to eliminate opponents with drawing hands in the same way you would with a single pair.

Start Cards

Flop Cards

Turn Card

The turn card is 2h. This is what's known as a "scary" flop, as a flush for an opponent is now a definite possibility. If someone now raises, throw in the towel. Otherwise, just call; you've still got a chance to win this hand, so if you can see the final card for one more bet, it's worth doing. If the river card doesn't make things any worse, and there are no raises, play the hand out.

However, if the river card is yet another heart, there are now four hearts on the board. With several opponents, a flush will be almost a certainty. Against one opponent, there's a chance of that player not having the flush, so if he or she doesn't raise, play the hand out.

Playing Sets on the Flop

As with the two-pair, these hands fall in one of two ways – two cards in the pocket and one on the board (concealed), or two cards on the board and one in the pocket (open).

While sets are an excellent hand (particularly concealed sets), they are far from being unbeatable. Many players slow-play this hand with the intention of getting as much money in the pot as possible. While in very rare situations this can be the correct play, usually it is incorrect. The problem is that they are leaving themselves open to the risk of someone completing a drawing hand.

The general rule, therefore, is that sets are played in the same way as pairs and two-pairs – aggressively.

Concealed Set

Of the two, concealed sets are by far the more powerful. If two of the cards are in the pocket, and only one is on the board, the opposition will have no idea that you have one. Let's look at a couple of examples of how to play them.

Start Cards

Flop Cards

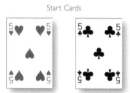

You've got 5-5 and another 5 on the board for your set. Otherwise, the flop is far from ideal. An opponent with a connector or a one-gapped connector, anywhere from an ace to a nine, will be looking to hit a straight. An opponent with two diamonds has a good chance of a flush. If either makes their hand, your set loses.

Therefore, you've got to force these players out of the game as soon as possible. The only way you can do that is by raising, thus making it too expensive for them to continue. If your raise is called, re-raise to keep the pressure on. Don't call – that will get you nowhere.

However, if the turn brings another low/middle card or diamond, or even worse, a low diamond, you will have to play the hand out by checking and calling. If you are raised, you should fold.

Here's an example of when it can be correct to slow-play a set.

Start Cards

Flop Cards

Firstly, you've hit the highest set. Secondly, there is little likelihood of being beaten by a straight or a flush *at the moment*. However, two more high cards, or two more low cards, on the turn and the river could give an opponent a straight. Similarly, two more hearts, clubs, or diamonds could see someone hitting a flush.

These are both long shots though, and as it stands you are winning. Assuming you have only one or two opponents, you can slow-play the hand and hope nothing dangerous falls on the turn and river. With three or more opponents, you would *not* slow-play; it would be too risky.

Open Set

This is a good hand, but not nearly as good as a concealed set.

Start Cards

Flop Cards

You have three kings for your set but only a 9 kicker. An opponent who is holding the fourth king and another card, ten or above, also has the same set but with a higher kicker. You could be beaten here already. Nevertheless, with a hand this good, you need to see some evidence of it. Raise. An opponent who does have a king is going to come straight back with a re-raise; there's your evidence. In this case, you should probably fold.

If the opponent is a loose player though, he or she may have a lower kicker than yours, or even just a two-pair. In this case, play the hand out by calling.

Playing Flush Draws on the Flop

Poker players love being dealt two suited cards. The chance of hitting a flush is suddenly on. Knowing how powerful this hand is, they will almost always draw to the river in the hope of making it. In most cases, though, they are making a mistake. It is a fact that consistently making this play represents a major leak in most players' games.

The first thing to be aware of is that you simply cannot play *any* suited cards. This is because the odds against making the flush are 16 to 1. The following is a typical example of a hand that should not be played.

You've been dealt 8d-5d and decide to go for a diamond flush. The flop cards are 2h-Qc-Kd, which gives you three diamonds. You need both the turn and river cards to be diamonds as well, and the chances of this happening are 1 in 23. So, effectively, you can discount the flush.

What else do you have? If you get an 8 or a 5, you've only got a low pair. If the board pairs, you've only got a low kicker to go with it. Also, there's no prospect of a straight. This hand was a loser right from the beginning. Let's see another example:

Here you kicked off with a top hand; Ac-Kc. As regards the flush, the flop has not been helpful; you still need two more clubs – the same 1 in 23 long-shot as in our first example. You can forget this.

However, you've flopped the top pair with a king kicker, and also a nut four-card straight draw.

Never play suited cards unless they are either high cards, or are connected. By doing this, if you miss the flush, you will still have other ways to hit a good hand.

Although you've missed the flush draw, you still have two more good options. The lesson, then, is that you only play suited pocket cards if they are either connected, or high cards (both, ideally). Let's see a couple of examples of how to play a flush draw:

Start Cards

Flop Cards

Your start cards are 3s-4s. The flop brings two more spades to give you a good chance of hitting the flush.

The problem is that even if you make it, it is only going to be a 4 high flush (you can discount the jack on the board as that is a community card). This means that if another player also makes the flush, his or hers will almost certainly be higher than yours. Therefore, you will have to play this one aggressively to force out any players who have spades in their hands. While it probably won't work, as most players will always try to hit a flush, it's the only thing you can do. If the turn or river does bring another spade to complete your flush and an opponent starts raising, then you can be fairly sure that this player has a higher flush than yours. In this case, you will have to fold.

Another example:

Start Cards

Flop Cards

This example is similar to the first with two exceptions: a) you have the nut flush draw, and b) you also have top pair with a chance of a set. If you raise, you risk your opponents folding, which you don't want because if you hit the flush, you're going to clean up. If you check, you risk the others checking as well and no money going in the pot. So in this situation, you call. This gets money in the pot and doesn't scare anyone off.

Playing Straight Draws on the Flop

Be very careful when playing a low-end straight. It is quite common for an opponent to have hit the high end of the straight.

A straight is a powerful hand, and as with flush draws, it is common to see people playing straight draws to the river in the hope of hitting one. However, don't lose sight of the fact that straights are not as good as flushes, so even if you hit one, it may well not be the winning hand. This is not an uncommon scenario.

The big danger with straights is hitting one on the low end and not being aware of (or forgetting) the possibility of someone hitting the high end. For example:

Start Cards

Flop Cards

You have 6-8-9-T, and need a 7 to complete the straight. However, if you do get it, it will be the low end of the straight. An opponent with J-Q (which is quite likely as they are high cards) will have a higher straight.

You have to raise here to drive out anyone holding either of these cards before they get a chance to hit the other one. If you are re-raised, you are probably beaten already and should fold.

In the example here, you have an inside straight (also known as a gutshot straight). The odds of making this on either the turn or river cards are 1 in 11. So you wouldn't be raising anyway. This hand, you play as cheaply as possible by calling and checking. Also, the pot odds will have to be greater than 11:1 to warrant the play.

Another example:

Start Cards

Flop Cards

Here, you have A-T and need a jack to complete a nut straight. As an added bonus, there is a king and a queen on the board, so there is a good chance that someone will have a high pair. If you do manage to hit the straight, you are likely to get some serious action. Also, there is no danger of a flush. So with nothing likely to beat your straight should you hit it, there is no need to raise; just check and call to string the opposition along.

Backdoor straight draws are hands that require both the turn and the river card to fall favorably.

An outside backdoor straight draw. It requires A-5 to complete it:

An inside backdoor straight draw. It requires J-K to complete it:

Drawing hands are best played from a late position. This allows you to fold pre-flop if most of the opposition has already done so. Remember, you need plenty of opponents to make these hands profitable.

The odds of hitting an outside backdoor straight are 1 in 38, and they are 1 in 71 for the inside backdoor straight. Not good.

Therefore, in most cases you should dump these hands unceremoniously. The only time you might play them is when they also have other possibilities. For example, the inside straight draw above where the hand also has A-A with a queen kicker.

At the risk of repeating ourselves, the most important thing to remember with drawing hands, be they straights, flushes, or sets, is that the pot odds must be high enough to make the play profitable over the long term. In most cases, this requires a good number of players to be in the game; if you get to the flop and have only one or two opponents, the odds just won't be there.

Repeating ourselves again, this is why these hands should usually be played from a late table position, as it's only from here that you will be able to see how many opponents you have.

Drawing Hands and Pot Odds

On the previous page we mentioned the importance of pot odds in relation to drawing hands. We'll show you a couple of simple examples to illustrate this point.

You are playing at a ten-seat $1.00/2.00 fixed-limit table, and holding Jd-8d. Five players fold and the other four bet. You call. This puts five bets into the pot – $5. The flop cards are dealt.

Start Cards   Flop Cards

Two players bet and the other two fold. This puts two more dollars in the pot – it now stands at $7. It's your turn to bet; what do you do? The only winning hand you're likely to make with these cards is a diamond flush. The chance of hitting it, though, is 1 in 23. The pot odds are 7:1 ($7 in the pot divided by the $1 you need to call). The odds against hitting the flush are much higher than the pot odds, so you fold.

If you are in a marginal situation with regard to the pot odds, don't forget to factor in the implied odds (see page 64).

Another example:

You are sitting at the same $1.00/2.00 table, and this time holding 8h-9c. Two players fold; the others, including you, all bet. This puts $8 in the pot. Then the flop is dealt.

Start Cards   Flop Cards

Four players fold, one raises, and two call the raise. Six more dollars go into the pot, making a total of $14.

You have an outside straight draw and the chance of hitting it is 1 in 5. The pot odds are 7:1 ($14 in the pot divided by the $2 you need to call the raise). The odds against making your hand are lower than the pot odds; therefore it's correct to bet.

Playing a Complete Hand on the Flop

Once in a blue moon, you will have the good fortune to flop a complete hand. This will be a straight or better.

Just to be clear: by a flopped complete hand, we mean that the three flop cards have completed the hand.

Flopped Straight

The first thing to be aware of is that you haven't cracked it yet. Your biggest danger now will be someone hitting a flush or a higher straight. How you play this hand depends on the strength of the straight and the flop cards. For example:

Start Cards

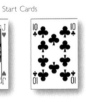

Flop Cards

You've caught the high end of the straight with your J-T. Your only worry here is the two spades which could be giving someone a flush draw. Therefore, you have to play this aggressively in order to force out anyone holding spades. Raise. If you are re-raised, re-raiser the raiser. This will, of course, cause lesser hands to fold, which you don't really want, but in this situation you are going to have to settle for whatever you can get.

Flopped Flush

Technically, you should do the same as with the straight, i.e. raise to drive out any flush draws. In reality though, this is unlikely to work. Consider the example below:

In the example opposite, the situation would be completely different if you were playing at a no-limit table. Then you could put in a really big bet so that the opposition would have to pay dearly to see the next card.

Start Cards

Flop Cards

Here you have a queen high flush. Anybody with the ace or king of diamonds needs just one more diamond to make a higher flush. It would be quite pointless raising in this situation, though, because with two cards still to come and a chance of hitting the nut flush, one extra bet is very unlikely to make them fold. Therefore, you may as well slow-play it and hope for the best.

Playing Overcards on the Flop

This is a situation where one, or both, of your pocket cards are higher than any card on the board.

For example:

Start Cards

Flop Cards

You have Ad-Jc, and were hoping for a high pair or a straight draw on the flop. Instead, all you've got is one overcard, and a backdoor inside straight draw. What do you do now?

Firstly, if you do play the hand and hit a pair, that's all you'll have – just a pair (if you hit a jack, you will be beaten by an opponent holding a queen).

Secondly, the board is showing a possible flush. So with two ways of being beaten even if you make a pair, you would have to fold. Note that this is usually the safest option with overcards.

However, if certain conditions are met, it can be correct to play overcards. For example:

Start Cards

Flop Cards

Here you have two overcards, either of which can make a top pair. The jack on the board also gives you an outside straight draw. Furthermore, the flop is safe in that it offers no straight or flush possibilities to the opposition.

In these conditions, and against one or two opponents, it would be worth taking a chance.

Playing a Full House on the Flop

A full house is a wonderful hand – usually. Sometimes, though, they are not so good. Consider the following example:

Be very wary of a full house when you have a pair in your pocket cards, as shown in the example opposite. This hand can be beaten by quads and by a full house. The former is unlikely but the latter is extremely likely.

Start Cards

Flop Cards

You have three jacks and two nines. However, this is not nearly as good a hand as it seems, and the reason is that the three jacks are all on the board. This means that every player still in the game has them as well.

Effectively, all you actually have is the pair of nines, and you would have to play the hand on this basis, as any player with a higher pair will beat you. Furthermore, a player fortunate enough to have the fourth jack will have quads.

All you can do in this situation is to raise in an attempt to knock out opponents with high cards that can make a higher pair than your 9-9. If you are re-raised, you are almost certainly up against another pair. It might be higher than yours or it might be lower, so you will have to play the hand out by checking and calling. You can't fold as you may well have the winning hand, but nor do you want to put any more in the pot than you have to, as you also have a fair chance of losing.

Another example in which we've rearranged the cards slightly:

Say your start cards were 9-J and the board was 9-9-J. This full house would be much weaker than the one opposite as an opponent with two jacks and any other pair would beat you. In this situation, you would have to play aggressively to deny opponents the chance of doing it.

Start Cards

Flop Cards

This is the full house you want – the nuts. With a jack in your start cards, quads are impossible. The hand is not unbeatable – an opponent with the last jack could still make a higher pair than 9-9, but in reality, it's very unlikely. This hand you can slow-play.

Playing the Turn

Another reason to raise on the turn is when the turn card looks threatening. For example, if the flop had two suits and the turn brings a third, then an opponent could have a flush draw. By raising, you are making it expensive for this player to see the river card, and hopefully he or she will fold.

As a general rule, if you haven't completed your hand by this stage, you should fold. By continuing, you are usually throwing good money after bad.

However, if you have, and have been playing the correct start cards, it should be the best hand, or close to it. If you are confident that it is, you should now be raising to get money in the pot. If you are re-raised, though, take a time-out to re-evaluate your hand and the board, checking that you haven't missed something. If you still can't see any obvious danger, re-raise the raiser. This is also likely to force out players who are hoping to complete a drawing hand on the river. Remember, this is your last chance to do this.

Aggressiveness at this stage is absolutely the best policy. This is not the time to mess about. Many players will fold good hands when faced with a bombardment of raises and re-raises. Think of it in this way: if you've been playing correctly by playing only good start cards, and from the correct positions, you will have saved yourself a huge number of single bets. What you are doing now is investing some of those bets on a good hand when it really counts.

The only times you should check or call are:

If you have doubts about the strength of your hand in relation to that of an opponent, either fold or call. Don't throw your money away by raising with what could well be a losing hand. Wait for a better opportunity.

- When you are drawing to a flush or straight (be sure that the pot odds are correct before putting a double bet in the pot. If not, continue only if you get a free card)

- When you've missed the hand you wanted and ended up with something not quite so good. For example, you may have been aiming at the high end of a straight and, instead, hit the low end. Whatever, if you aren't confident the hand is going to win but think it has a chance, play it out by calling and checking. Don't pay any more than you have to, though. If someone raises, fold

- When you have a nut hand. In this case, slow-play the hand to ensure as many of your opponents as possible stay in to the end. You want to give them every opportunity to hit their hands

Playing the River

When the river card flips over, you know for sure what your best hand is. In most cases, though, it will be no better than it was on the turn, or even the flop.

If you've been drawing to a flush or straight because the pot odds warranted it, you now either have it or you don't. Your decision is clear-cut: bet or fold (against one opponent, it may be worth trying to bluff the other player out of it by raising).

If you already had your best hand on the turn and were betting aggressively, re-evaluate the board with regard to how the river card may have improved your opponents' hands. Things to take note of are:

- A third suit, indicating that a flush is possible. If a player who was previously calling and checking now puts in a raise, this is the time to either fold a straight or lower, or just call

- A pair on the board. In this situation, you may now be up against a set (especially if it is a high pair), a full house, or quads. If an opponent raises and you hold a two-pair or less, fold. Otherwise, call

- A card that connects other board cards. This increases the possibility of a straight. Of course, if you already have a straight beaten, you're going to love this

A good rule for river play is that you should rarely fold a hand that has a reasonable chance of winning. This is especially true in low-limit poker where players are likely to play with literally anything. If in doubt, just call and check to see the hand out cheaply, but don't fold it unless someone is raising aggressively. Surrendering a winning hand is not a smart move.

Be very wary of getting involved in a raising war with two or more opponents when you are holding nothing higher than a pair. It's very tempting to play a pair of aces to the bitter end, but against two opponents who are betting aggressively, it's usually a costly mistake. In this situation, you will almost always be beaten by a two-pair or a set. This is one instance where you should fold.

Short-Hand Play

Playing short-hand is when you face six opponents or fewer. This can be at a ten-seat table where several seats are unoccupied, a six-seat, or a two-seat table. Whichever, the fact that you are facing fewer opponents means that you must adjust your strategy accordingly.

Many pots in short-hand games are won with high pairs and two-pairs. In fact, it's not unusual to see a high card take the pot.

With less opposition, hands take on a higher value. Many games are won with a pair, or a two-pair. Many start cards that you would fold in a ten-player game are worth playing short-hand. Middle pairs (7-7 to T-T) should be played in the same way as you would play high pairs at a ten-seat table. Also, kickers are less of an issue as the chances of an opponent having a higher card are lower.

Drawing hands, however, are much less valuable. The reason is that with fewer opponents, the pot odds are often not high enough to warrant playing these hands. Thus, you should only play connectors and suited cards that have a high face value, giving you the chance of a high pair as well; middle and low cards should be folded. Because of this, don't let a straight or flush draw on the board put you off playing a good pair or two-pair. The chances of being beaten by a drawing hand are much less than in a ten-player game.

A very important factor in short-handed poker is your style of play. Aggression is the keyword. Players who call frequently will find it tough going as they are going to find themselves being raised constantly.

You will find that opponents bluff much more than they do in long-hand games. If you are the type of player who finds it difficult to call a raise with anything other than a top hand, you will struggle to survive.

Bluffing is a much used tactic in short-hand poker and you need to be able to deal with this – if you allow yourself to be intimidated, you will lose many pots to players with lesser hands. This makes it very important to study the way your opponents play. If you know which of them bluff, and when, and which don't, not only will you be able to call a bluff, you will be able to use this tactic yourself.

You also need to be aware of the danger of being beaten by the blinds. These come round much more quickly than in a ten-player game, and players who sit and wait for the best hands are going to lose a lot of their money in the blinds. Thus, you will need to win pots more frequently, which in turn means playing more hands.

No-Limit Texas Hold'em

Often described as the "Cadillac" of poker by professionals, no-limit poker is like no other poker game you will play. While the basic concepts of good strategy, such as correct start card selection, also apply to no-limit, there are a range of other factors, knowledge of which is essential.

Beginners are advised to stay well away from no-limit. However, should they decide to try their luck at it, the advice in this chapter will stand them in very good stead.

Covers

Chapter Seven

Introduction

No-limit poker is exactly the same as fixed-limit, with one exception – the betting structure. In a no-limit game, players have complete freedom of choice regarding the size of the bets they make. If they want to risk their entire stack on one bet, they can (and frequently do). This single factor introduces a number of elements that makes no-limit a much more difficult game to master. These include:

If you like excitement, no-limit is the game for you. There's no denying that fixed-limit can be a drudge – you can play this for hours and be no better off than when you started. In no-limit, you can double your stack in a single hand.

Skill

Because bets can be huge, no-limit provides little room for error. Mistakes in fixed-limit that cost you two or three bets can be far more expensive in no-limit. Consistently bad play (or bad luck) can bankrupt you in a very short space of time. Consequently, you need to be a far more proficient player to survive in this game.

Psychology

The ever-present threat of being suddenly faced with a huge bet to stay in the game can have a dramatic influence on some players' behavior. Some will fold winning hands rather than get into a confrontation with an aggressive opponent. Their fear of the big raise makes them play too conservatively.

Stack Size

A player with a stack twenty times the size of yours can keep going all in against you with trash hands. Even if the first few miss, eventually this opponent is going to pull a lucky card and bust you. There is simply no defence against this. If you keep folding, in many cases you will be folding the winning hand, and if you bet, this player will get you in the end. This is a bit of a simplification but it serves to illustrate the point – players with a small stack are at a big disadvantage.

Bluffing

In fixed-limit, the bluff is a weak play as it costs only a small bet to call it. In no-limit, it is a powerful weapon that wins many pots with inferior hands. Knowing how, and when, to use the bluff is a distinguishing feature of the good no-limit player.

Aggression/Initiative

The player in control of the betting, i.e. making the big bets, has the initiative; opponents are responding to his or her actions.

Start Cards

Start card requirements for no-limit are slightly different from those in fixed-limit, and one reason for this is the fact that drawing hands have less value. Playing these hands will have you folding to a large bet much more often than in low-limit because it will be too expensive to continue with the hand.

Also, very often no-limit games don't get as far as the river (or even the turn) due to the volatility of the betting. In this situation, anyone playing suited or connected start cards in the hope of making a straight or a flush won't get a chance to complete it, and thus will have wasted their bets. Consequently, playing this type of hand can be an expensive hobby in no-limit. A lot depends on the opposition: if they are mainly the passive type, drawing hands can be worth playing. It only takes one or two aggressive players, though, to make playing drawing hands an unprofitable exercise.

Flush and straight draws are not as good in no-limit as they are in fixed-limit. You will have less chance to complete them, and even if you do, the pot odds will often not be high enough to make them pay over the long term.

There is also the risk of being tempted to call a large bet due to inexperience, or simply making a mistake. In fixed-limit it won't be too costly; in no-limit it may be very expensive, particularly if you then make the second-best hand and decide to play on with it. This is what's known as being "trapped" and it usually stems from poor start card selection.

The following table lists the recommended start cards for no-limit Hold'em:

Sticking to the start cards in the table opposite will keep you out of many awkward and, potentially, dangerous situations.

Playable Start Cards
Early Position
A-A, K-K, Q-Q, A-Ks, A-Qs, A-Ko, A-Qo
Middle Position
J-J, T-T, 9-9, A-Js, A-Ts, K-Qs, K-Js, Q-Js, A-Jo, A-To, K-Qo, K-Jo, plus all the early position hands
Late Position
8-8, 7-7, 6-6, 5-5, 4-4, 3-3, 2-2, A-5s, A-4s, A-3s, A-2s, K-Ts, K-9s, Q-Ts, J-Ts, K-To, Q-Jo, Q-To, plus early and middle position hands
A – Ace, K – King, Q – Queen, J – Jack, T – Ten, 2-9 – card value, x – unknown card, s – same suit, o – different suits

Pre-Flop Strategy

The key factor in pre-flop play is selection of good start cards. While this is important in all forms of poker, getting this wrong in no-limit can be very costly.

Because of the danger of being faced with a huge bet, you need to be even more selective with your start cards than you would in a fixed-limit game. The big danger in no-limit is getting yourself trapped with the second-best hand. Remember, the more money you commit to a pot, the harder it becomes to write it off; you will always be tempted to see just one more card in the hope of improving your hand. This is fatal in no-limit. It's going to happen of course, but by playing only the right start cards, you will be limiting the times it does.

Early Position

Playable hands are: A-A, K-K, Q-Q, A-Ks, A-Ko, A-Qs, A-Qo.

With A-A to Q-Q, you bet hard. These are top hands pre-flop but are more likely to be beaten the longer the game goes on. As in fixed-limit, the goal is to knock out as much of the competition pre-flop as possible.

The ability to make huge bets provides a wonderful opportunity to maximize the pay-off from top pairs. You just need someone with a slightly lower pair to call your bet (and not improve their hand).

How much do you raise by, though? Some players would go all in with A-A hoping one opponent will accept the challenge. In this situation, they would be a hot favorite to win the pot. You can do this yourself – it's not a bad play; only do it with A-A, though. What's more likely to happen, however, is that everyone will simply fold; all you'll have won is the blinds money, which is not much reward for the best hand. So to make it worthwhile going all in with A-A, you really need a couple of loose players at the table, one of whom is likely to call the bet.

What you want to do then is bet an amount that will muscle all but one or two of your opponents out of the game. Typically, this will be two or three times the size of the higher betting limit ($40-60 in a $10.00/20.00 game). This will make most players fold.

If you are re-raised by a large amount, fold anything lower than K-K. With A-A or K-K, re-raise the raiser. If the re-raise is low, call with Q-Q. If someone goes all in, or a second player re-raises, fold everything bar A-A.

With A-Ks, A-Ko, A-Qs and A-Qo, just bet and see what develops. A small raise you can call with A-Ks and A-Ko. Fold the A-Qs and A-Qo. Fold all these hands to a large raise.

Middle Position

Playable hands are: J-J, T-T, 9-9, A-Js, A-Ts, K-Qs, K-Js, Q-Js, A-Jo, A-To, K-Qo, K-Jo, plus all the early position hands.

Making a large bet from a middle position will usually buy you a better table position for the later betting rounds. In no-limit this is a much more effective strategy than it is in fixed-limit.

In middle position, you should play A-A, K-K, Q-Q in exactly the same way you would in early position. You can also raise with J-J, T-T, 9-9, A-Ks, A-Ko, A-Qs and A-Qo. Quite apart from limiting the competition, you will also be buying yourself a better table position.

If your J-J to 9-9 is re-raised, re-raise the raiser. You really need to win with these hands before the flop, as afterwards they will be vulnerable to overcards. If your opponent(s) persist and re-raise yet again, you are probably beaten and should fold. While these are good cards and you should make a decent attempt to win the pot with them, you should back down in the face of determined opposition.

With A-Ks, A-Ko, A-Qs and A-Qo, you should fold to any re-raise.

The lesser hands, from A-Js downwards, are worth seeing the flop with if you can do so cheaply by calling and checking. These often turn into high pairs and high two-pairs. In the face of any raises, you should fold them, though.

Late Position

Playable hands are: 8-8, 7-7, 6-6, 5-5, 4-4, 3-3, 2-2, A-5s, A-4s, A-3s, A-2s, K-Ts, K-9s, Q-Ts, J-Ts, K-To, Q-Jo, Q-To, plus all the early and middle position hands.

Because it is less common to see straights and flushes in no-limit, low and middle pairs that can turn into a set are worth more than they are in fixed-limit.

In late position, you have the big advantage of having seen all your opponents' moves. This allows you to play many more hands than you would in the earlier positions.

Play A-A to 9-9 as already described. With these hands, you are looking to tempt one opponent into calling your bet and then re-raise that player out of the game. The goal is to win the pot then and there.

In no-limit, low and middle pairs are more valuable than they are in fixed-limit.

The reason for this is that straights and flushes are less common in no-limit as the pot odds are often not good enough to make them worth playing. With low and middle pairs, you are looking to hit a set. These hands (particularly concealed sets) are the ideal hands in no-limit and win huge pots. If you hit your set, in most cases you'll have the winning hand.

While sets are more powerful hands than they are in fixed-limit, the odds against hitting one are exactly the same. Don't chase after them. If you hit one on the flop, fine; if you don't, fold.

Some professionals advocate raising pre-flop with any pair to build up the pot in case the set hits. However, you must remember that the chance of making this hand on the flop from a pair is 1 in 7.5. Bearing this in mind, you're probably better off seeing the flop as cheaply as possible with middle and low pairs. If there's a small raise in front of you, call, but fold to a large raise, or a re-raise.

Notice that we do not advise playing low or middle connectors, suited or otherwise. These are drawing hands, and as previously stated, the pot odds, generally, do not allow you to make a profit with them.

A-2s to A-5s are worth playing, as not only do they give you a chance of a straight or a flush, you can also hit a top pair. Plus, if you hit a low pair or set, you'll have the highest kicker.

Pre-Flop Tips

Bets need to be substantial. If you're attempting to knock out the opposition, either to win the pot outright or to limit the competition, pre-flop bets need to be significant in comparison to the pot. You must present your opponents with a powerful incentive to fold. Half-hearted attempts that fail often have serious repercussions in the later stages of the game.

If you make a big bet to try and knock out opponents, make sure it is big enough to do the job. If it isn't and they don't fold, very often this will be money lost.

You must know the opposition. For example, be wary of a tight player who suddenly makes a large bet. This usually indicates A-A or K-K, so folding is usually the sensible option. On the other hand, weak or loose players can be called with lesser hands.

Try trapping an opponent. The usual procedure with A-A or K-K is to raise the pot. Do the opposite once in a while by just calling. Then, assuming you get a safe flop, throw in a large bet. What you want is just one opponent to bite. Then raise that player big-time. In most cases they'll then fold and you've won yourself a nice bet (see page 110 for more on trapping).

Post-Flop Strategy

Aggressive bluffing post-flop will steal many pots. However, you must pick players who allow themselves to be bullied. Also, you must be able to let the hand go if the bluff doesn't work.

The mechanics of post-flop play, e.g. reading the board, are no different from those in fixed-limit, so we're not going to repeat ourselves by explaining how to play each type of hand as we did in Chapter 6. Rather, we'll just highlight some pertinent points.

In no-limit, the decisions you make here are far more critical than in fixed-limit as, potentially, there is a lot more at stake.

If you don't think your hand measures up, you've got two choices: either drop it or bet hard (bluff). Calling is not usually a good move in no-limit for the simple reason that it puts no pressure on the opposition – something you should be looking to do as often as possible. The only time you should be calling is when you've flopped a monster hand. In this situation, you will be slow-playing to let as many players as possible see the turn and river cards and, hopefully, hit a lesser hand.

If you do decide to bluff it out, your decision must be based on the number of your opponents and how they are likely to respond. Obviously, the more opposition you have, the riskier this move becomes, so only do it against one or two opponents. They must also be opponents of the type who are likely to fold under pressure.

If you get it wrong and are called or raised, you have to let the hand go, regardless of how much you have invested in the pot. While this type of play is not going to win every time, what it will do is get you a lot more action when you do have the best hand. If your opponents see that you take risks occasionally, they will be more inclined to call your bets.

Straight and flush draws you should drop if the flop doesn't give you two of the cards you need. Even if it does, you will need to consider the pot odds to determine if it's worthwhile paying to see the turn card.

We mentioned earlier that sets can be a killer-hand in no-limit and this is true. However, it is a big mistake to chase them consistently to the turn and river. Generally, if the third card doesn't fall on the flop, fold the hand. It can be worth taking a chance, though, if a large pot is up for grabs.

The All-In Bet

Players go all-in when they put all their money in the pot. This is the most powerful move that can be made in poker.

The tactic is most commonly used in tournaments, often in the early stages, either to build a large stack quickly or to rebuild a dangerously low stack. Players in the latter situation are in imminent danger of being swallowed up by the blinds (see page 115), and so need to do something drastic to get back in the game. As soon as they get a half-decent hand, they'll go all-in. They've got little to lose by doing this – if they win they double-up (double their stack) and are back in the game; if they lose, they're out, which they would soon have been anyway because of the blinds.

Should you call an all-in bet or make one yourself in a cash game, though? In the right circumstances, most definitely. "Right circumstances" would be defined as:

Pre-Flop

- With A-A, against any opponent regardless of table position

- With K-K, in late position only, assuming: a) no more than one player is all-in (if two players are all-in, you have to assume one of them has A-A), and b) the opponent isn't a tight player (tight players rarely go all-in with less than A-A)

Post-Flop

- Against any opponent when you are holding a set, assuming: a) it is a concealed set (no pair on the board to give possible quads or a full house to opponents), and b) there is no flush or straight draw on the board

- When you are holding a nut straight, assuming: a) there is no flush draw, and b) the board isn't paired

- When you are holding a nut flush and the board isn't paired

The exception to the above is when a short-stacked player goes all in (see bottom margin note).

When just one player calls an all-in bet, the betting in that game is over. Any remaining community cards are revealed and the player with the best hand takes the pot. However, if two or more players call an all-in bet, the game carries on and a second pot (known as a sidepot) is created for these players. If the all-in player wins the game, he or she takes the pot they were involved in, i.e. the main pot. The sidepot goes to the player with the next best hand.

When a short-stacked player goes all-in this is often an all-or-nothing move born of desperation, and the player may be holding nothing better than two high cards. In this situation, you can call with any pair.

Bluffing

In no-limit, the power of the unlimited bet makes bluffing a much more potent weapon. It can also make it a double-edged sword, though; if the bluff is called, you will lose more. Because of this danger, you need to pick the right time and the right opponent – indiscriminate bluffing will get you nowhere.

Essentially, a bluff is playing the opponent rather than the cards. You are gambling that your perception of other players is accurate. If it is, and they fold, the cards are irrelevant.

The opponent is probably the most important factor. Aggressive players who don't like backing down, and maniacs who can't resist betting, should not be bluffed. Unless you are prepared to go the whole hog with an all-in bet, they will often call you.

Against tight players, you should only try a bluff if you act after them: you need to see them play first – if they make a good-sized bet then they've hit a good hand and you can forget the idea. If they call or check then go ahead.

The ideal opponent to bluff is the tight-passive player. These people really shouldn't be playing no-limit; they are simply too timid for their own good. Usually, they are more concerned with protecting their stack than they are in building it up.

With regard to suitable situations in which to bluff, please refer to pages 69-70.

Being caught out with a bluff occasionally is not a bad thing as it will induce opponents to take more chances against you.

In no-limit, bluffing can win money in a more roundabout way. Obviously, you can't expect to win every bluff; you are going to get caught out now and again. When you do, even though you've lost some money, there is a positive side effect. By showing the opposition that you are prepared to take risks, you are creating a loose (or less tight, at any rate) table image. When you do get the monster hand, the opposition are more likely to call your bets and your big hand will win a lot more money.

The trick is not to lose money overall on the bluffs. Even if you just break even on them (and by carefully selecting the opponents to bluff, you should achieve at least that), your winnings on the big hands will be increased considerably.

Being seen as a timid player is the worst table image you can have in no-limit. The occasional bluff will soon dispel that image and make the opposition treat you with much more respect.

Trapping

This is a situation in which you think you have the winning hand but an opponent has an even better hand. Because you expect to win, you keep betting; by the time the truth begins to dawn, it's too late. If you fold, you have to surrender all the money you've put in the pot; if you continue you're going to lose even more – you've trapped yourself in a no-win situation.

In most cases, players trap themselves rather than being trapped deliberately by an opponent. This is usually the result of playing bad start cards. For example, you play with 7-T and the flop brings 6-T-T giving you a set with a 7 kicker. An opponent, however, is holding J-T and so has the same set but with a higher kicker. If you had folded this hand at the beginning (as you should have done) you wouldn't have got yourself in this mess.

Certain hands have a much greater potential than others for trapping players. Any high card with a low card (A-4, K-3, for example), particularly if unsuited, is liable to make only a second- or third-best hand.

To trap an opponent deliberately, you do a reverse-bluff with the intention of representing a strong hand as a weak one. Three conditions are necessary for this:

- The opposition must be good players who study and analyze their opponents' moves

- You need to be perceived as a player who can be expected to make the occasional risky play

- You need a top hand. Pre-flop it will be A-A or K-K. Post-flop, you should have at least a set or a straight

Trap hands are known as "dominated hands" because of the likelihood of an opponent having a similar but better one. For example: you have A-5 and an opponent has A-Q. Your A-5 is dominated because you need to hit at least a pair to win. If you don't, the A-Q will win without any improvement.

With these conditions met, you now make a much higher bet than is normal for you. The good players are likely to view this as an attempt to bluff them out of the pot, and thus put you on a weak hand. Being good players, they will do the correct thing and call (or even raise) your bet. By doing so they have allowed themselves to be trapped.

It is difficult to trap weak or timid players because they are fixated with their cards; they don't think about what the opposition may be up to. Making a big bet will just convince them that you have a big hand and they'll fold. It'll never occur to them that you may be bluffing.

The Stack

The amount of cash you have on the table – your stack – is much more important in no-limit than it is in fixed-limit.

To a certain degree, players who have a high stack in relation to their opponents have a "power" advantage (it's like having an army: a general with 10,000 troops is going to be much more powerful than one with 1,000).

Never sit down at a no-limit table with a small stack. Aggressive players will take advantage.

High-stacked players command respect when they make a big bet and will often win pots unopposed, as opponents will be fearful of being faced with an all-in bet. Rather than risk a potentially expensive confrontation, they will back down. High-stacked players can try different stratagems and generally mix up their play. Basically, a high stack allows you to play optimum poker.

Contrast this with short-stacked players, who are inevitably under constant pressure. They will be called much more frequently because they do not have any "power". Even if they go all in, it's not a major threat to a high-stacked opponent. To avoid busting-out, they will often play negative poker and, consequently, are likely to see their stack dwindle further.

Another big problem with being short-stacked is that if you do manage to hit a monster hand, you won't be able to maximize the pay-off from it. You may have the great frustration of an opponent also hitting a good, but lesser, hand and being prepared to bet heavily on it. If you've only got $10, that's all you're going to get from such an opponent – if you'd had $100, however ....

To limit the big advantage of a large stack, all poker rooms set a maximum buy-in amount for no-limit tables. Otherwise, a player could put down a huge stack of, say, $50,000 and simply blitz the opposition out of existence.

When playing no-limit poker be prepared to see your stack take wide swings in both directions. If you are of a nervous disposition, you might find this hard to handle.

If you play no-limit correctly (selective aggression), your stack is going to see-saw wildly (but with an upward trend). You must have an adequate amount in front of you in order to ride out the "downs", and, also, avoid the disadvantages of being short-stacked. For these reasons, it is a good idea to buy in for the maximum amount when joining a no-limit table. This starts you off with an immediate advantage.

Common No-Limit Mistakes

Of all the mistakes players make in no-limit poker, bluffing (either too much or too little) is probably the most common. If you can't get this right, you will find it difficult to win.

Not Bluffing (or Not Bluffing Enough)

This is one of the biggest mistakes. The bluff is a player's best weapon in no-limit and not using it is a major error. It's like going into battle with a machine-gun but only using a bow and arrow.

Bluffing Too Much

By bluffing, you are telling the opposition that you have a good hand. However, good hands don't come along that often; bluff too much and your opponents simply won't believe you.

Overvaluing Pairs

This happens in fixed-limit as well, but is much more dangerous in no-limit. The danger is calling large bets with the second-best hand.

Under-Betting

Quite simply, if you don't make large enough bets, your opponents will have no reason to fold their hands. This mistake will sting you big-time in the later stages of a game.

Overdoing the All-In Bet

A successful all-in move is the quickest and easiest way to win serious money at poker. The reverse is also true. You need to pick the times you do this carefully.

The other big mistake is concentrating more on your cards than you do on your opponents. If you can get a good "read" on how they play, you will often be able to win with weak hands that would have no chance in fixed-limit.

Not "Letting Go"

Continuing with a hand that's probably beaten. A typical example would be turning up 7-7 and seeing the flop, hoping for a set. If another 7 doesn't come, you should fold unless the pot odds are good. Many players will draw to the river in this situation, whatever the pot odds.

Playing the Cards Rather than the Players

An absolutely essential part of no-limit is knowing your opponents. Nearly every decision you make should be based on your observations of how they play. By doing this you will make far fewer mistakes, and be able to induce them into errors of judgement. If you ignore this aspect and play only on the basis of what cards you have, you are going to miss out on many good opportunities, and, also, find yourself being manipulated by the opposition.

Tournaments

In this chapter we investigate poker tournaments. There are several different types and we take a look at all of them.

To win poker tournaments, you need to play with a different strategy from that you'd use in cash games. This chapter shows you how to do it.

Covers

Introduction

Tournaments are rapidly becoming one of the most popular forms of poker – many people play nothing else. One of the reasons for this is the increasingly extensive television coverage they are now receiving. Another is the fact that you "know where you are" with them. You know exactly how much it's going to cost to enter and you have a good idea of how long it will take.

So what exactly is a poker tournament? Basically, it's a game of elimination. Each entrant buys in for a fixed amount and the total buy-in forms the prize pool. In addition, the poker room charges each entrant a fee that, typically, is 10% of the buy-in (this is how the poker room makes its money).

As the tournament progresses, players lose their chips and are eliminated until just one remains. Typically, this player will win 20-30% of the pool.

There are many different types of tournament and the main ones include:

- Heads-up
- Multi-table (MTT)
- Single-table (STT)
- Sit-and-go
- Rebuy
- Satellite
- Freeroll
- Private

All online poker rooms have most of the tournament types listed above on offer. Some, like the multi-table affairs, have a fixed starting time and are pre-announced. The sit-and-go type, on the other hand, are ready as soon as the last player has taken a seat.

Tournaments are available for all the variations of poker found online. The most popular is Texas Hold'em (both fixed- and no-limit) but you will also find them for Seven-Card Stud and Omaha.

Types of Tournament

Multi-table tournaments are usually over in a matter of hours. For example, a 2500 player tournament will last for about four hours. Over such a short period, luck becomes a very important factor. If the cards aren't falling, even the best players will struggle to survive.

Multi-Table (MTT)

If you want to win serious money playing poker, multi-table tournaments are the way to do it. However, there will be several hundred, or even thousands, of other players all with the same thing in mind. You will need skill and a very large slice of luck to come out on top. Indeed, luck is without doubt the single most important factor in any given tournament. Yes, you need to be a good player (which is why the same players consistently reach the final stages of the World Series of Poker – see page 175), but to actually win also requires that good fortune is on your side on that particular day.

Here's how they work:

The first step is to register for the tournament, at which time the buy-in and entry fee is deducted from your account.

When the registration period is over, each entrant is allocated a seat at a table. Using a 200-player tournament as an example, there will be 20 tables, each seating ten players. When the tournament is due to begin, a window will flash up on your screen with the table at which you've been seated.

One of the main differences between a standard cash game and a tournament is the way the blinds are structured. In a tournament, they increase remorselessly: this means players have to win pots to stay in the game. If they don't, the blinds will swallow them up eventually.

The purpose is to prevent players just sitting on their stacks and waiting for their opponents to be eliminated.

Each player is allocated the same number of chips, usually 1500. At the beginning of the tournament (level one), the blinds are at a very low level, typically 10/20. However, at specific intervals (these vary, but we'll use a typical figure of 15 minutes as an example), they increase. When this happens the tournament is said to have moved to level two. 15 minutes later, the blinds increase again and the tournament is at level three. After four hours, the tournament will be at level 16, and the blinds will be in the region of 4000/8000.

As players lose their chips and are eliminated, remaining players are moved to different tables and redundant tables are closed. This is known as rebalancing. When only ten players remain, they are all seated at the final table.

Play continues until all but one has been eliminated.

Satellite tournaments offer a cheap route into the big money tournaments.

Satellites

A satellite tournament is basically a small tournament within a large tournament. There is no cash prize; instead, the winner gets a free seat at the next stage (known as a super-satellite) of the main tournament. The goal is to win through to the final stages (or final table) of the tournament. The advantage of the satellite is that, for a very small initial entry fee, it is possible to end up at a table where the buy-in can be several thousand dollars. The most well-known example of this is the World Series of Poker Championship. To buy a seat in the final stages of this tournament costs some $10,000. If you can get there via satellites, though, it will cost you a fraction of that amount.

Most of the major online poker rooms run satellite tournaments that lead to the WSOP.

Rebuys and Add-Ons

Rebuy tournaments are those in which players can buy more chips if they wish to. So if you lose your initial stack, rather than busting out of the tournament, you can buy another stack. Usually, there is no limit to the number of times you can do this.

Many players will do an immediate rebuy. This doubles their stack and gives them an advantage over the players who don't. However, they will have invested twice as much.

However, rebuys are restricted to specific periods (known as rebuy periods, surprisingly). Typically, these last an hour and usually occur in the early stages of the tournament. In some cases, the rebuy period is not time-limited but will be specified in terms of levels of the tournament. For example, rebuys may be allowed in levels one, two, and three.

You don't need to have lost your initial stack before you can rebuy. Some poker rooms allow you to rebuy if your stack is equal to or less than the initial stack. This means that you can do an immediate rebuy before the first card is dealt (see margin note). Sometimes, a rebuy is permitted only when a player's stack has dropped to half, or less, of its initial size. The conditions vary according to the poker room and the tournament.

Add-ons are one-off opportunities to purchase more chips, and are offered at intervals throughout the tournament. There are no restrictions as there are with rebuys. Regardless of your stack size, you can buy more.

The big advantage of STT's is that they are very quick. You also have a much greater chance of finishing in the prize money.

Single-Table (STT)

These tournaments are probably the most popular of all. Usually, they are restricted to ten players, and as soon as the last player has taken a seat, the tournament begins.

The beauty of single-table tournaments (and one reason that they're so popular) is that they are quick – most are completed within an hour. This means that you don't have to take the entire afternoon off as you would with a multi-table tournament.

The other big advantage is that you only have to beat seven players to finish in the money. Therefore, your chances of at least recouping the buy-in are good. The prize money is as follows:

- First place takes 50% of the prize pool
- Second place takes 30%
- Third place takes 20%

There are also plenty of these tournaments running. As soon as you've finished one, you can sit down at another.

Heads-Up

Heads-up poker is very difficult to master. See page 125 for more details on this.

In a heads-up tournament, players are pitched against single opponents. Winners advance to the next stage of the tournament where they face another single opponent. At no time are there more than two players at a table.

Private

Most poker rooms allow you to set up a private tournament in which only players specified by you can take part.

It can be any type of game (Hold'em, Omaha, Seven-Card Stud, etc), and you can specify the tournament's parameters yourself. These include the buy-in, the blinds levels, the prize distribution, and the number of starting chips.

You will need to enter all the details in an online form provided by the poker room to set it up. When you are ready to run the tournament, you normally need to advise the poker room by email or telephone.

Always check the freeroll tournament's cash-out requirements. You will sometimes need to play some hands for real money before the site lets you take the money out.

Freeroll

A freeroll is a tournament where there is no cash buy-in, but the winners receive cash or some other kind of worthwhile prize (for example, free entry to a cash tournament).

While the poker rooms lose money on these events, they offer them for two reasons: a) as a means of enticing people into their sites, and b) to reward loyal players (it's an incentive to keep their custom).

To play in any freeroll tournament, a player must have an account at the site in question and also, in most cases, must have made a previous cash deposit and played a certain number of raked hands. Poker rooms that insist on this typically award players points depending on the number of raked hands played, which can then be used as the freeroll buy-in. However, there are still a few that don't insist on this.

The poker rooms are not in the business of giving money away, so, not surprisingly, prizes tend to be less than spectacular. Typical figures range from $20 to $500. The higher the money on offer, the more entrants there will be. It's quite common to see several thousand players battling it out for the higher amounts.

We advise you not to waste too much of your time on freerolls. With such huge numbers of opponents, the chances of winning are extremely remote.

Are they worth it? Well, this depends on why you play poker. Certainly, they can be an enjoyable way of passing an hour or two, with the added bonus of a possible prize at the end. If you are thinking of them as a way of making money, though, think again. Typically, winners get about 25% of the prize pool, so in a $200 tournament, the first prize will be in the region of $50. This is not much to show for what will take several hours of your time (assuming you win, of course).

From a practical viewpoint, their only real worth is as an introduction to real money tournament play. As with all free-money tables though, you have to take what you see with a pinch of salt. Players do the craziest things in freerolls. If you play them often enough, some of this craziness might start rubbing off on you and become part of your real money game.

In essence, then, freerolls are fun and, for newcomers to tournament play, can be instructive to a certain degree.

Prize Money

When a tournament is over, the prize money is distributed and automatically credited to the winning players' accounts. The table below shows how prize pools are split for tournaments of all sizes. The figures are percentages (and are approximate).

One of the latest online tournament trends is the "speed" or "turbo" tournament. In these, the blinds increase every five minutes or so. You can even find some where they increase every two or three minutes.

Some tournaments incorporate a bounty feature. This adds another element to a standard tournament by having some players carry a bounty on their heads. If you eliminate any of them from the tournament you will receive a bounty bonus.

Players	1 to 30	31 to 50	51 to 100	101 to 200	201 to 400	401 to 600	601 to 800	801 to 1000	1001 plus
1st	50.00	40.00	30.00	27.50	25.00	25.00	25.00	25.00	22.50
2nd	30.00	24.00	20.00	17.00	16.00	15.00	14.50	14.00	12.50
3rd	20.00	16.00	12.00	11.50	10.50	9.50	9.25	9.00	8.50
4th		12.00	9.25	8.50	8.00	7.00	6.75	6.50	6.50
5th		8.00	7.50	7.25	7.00	6.00	5.75	5.50	5.25
6th			6.25	5.75	5.50	5.00	4.75	4.50	4.25
7th			5.25	4.50	4.50	4.00	3.75	3.50	3.25
8th			4.25	3.00	3.00	3.00	2.75	2.50	2.25
9th			3.25	2.00	1.75	1.75	1.75	1.50	1.50
10th			2.25	2.00	1.25	1.25	1.25	1.00	1.00
11-15				1.20	0.95	0.95	0.95	0.90	0.85
16-20				1.10	0.75	0.75	0.75	0.70	0.65
21-30					0.50	0.50	0.50	0.50	0.45
31-40					0.40	0.35	0.35	0.35	0.35
41-50						0.30	0.30	0.30	0.30
51-60						0.25	0.25	0.25	0.25
61-70							0.20	0.20	0.20
71-90							0.15	0.15	0.15
91-110								0.10	0.10
111-150									0.10

From the table we can see that the more entrants there are in a tournament, the more ways the prize pool is split. We can also see that to be in the prize money it is necessary to finish in the final 10% approximately.

However, to win a worthwhile amount of money it is usually necessary to finish in the final 3 or 4%.

Chip Stacks

It is very important to know how you are doing in comparison with the opposition. This is especially so in the later stages when you are getting near the money-paying positions. Keep an eye on this as it will affect your strategy.

The number of chips you have is very important. This may seem an obvious statement, but we are talking about knock-out tournaments here. Run out of chips in a cash game and there is nothing to stop you buying some more. In a tournament, however, with no chips you're out of the game (unless it's a rebuy).

The size of your stack also has a big influence on the way you play, and there are several reasons for this:

Firstly, in a multi-table tournament where you are facing hundreds or even thousands of opponents, it is essential to know where you stand in relation to the opposition. You may have the most chips at your table, but what about all the other tables? Are you in 8th place overall, or is it 800th? If it's 8th then you are doing well and may decide to consolidate your position by playing conservatively for a while. If it's 800th though, you may well need to do the opposite in an attempt to improve your position.

Secondly, in a tournament a large stack buys you power. It allows you to play more aggressively and make larger bets. You will be able to intimidate opponents who are short-stacked.

Thirdly, if you are short-stacked you face another, more relentless, opponent: the blinds. Unless you increase your stack, and soon, they will eat you up. In a cash game this isn't an issue as the blinds are always at the same level. In a tournament, however, they increase every time the game moves up a level. You will be much more susceptible to the vagaries of luck, and vulnerable to the power-plays of opponents with larger stacks. In this situation, your strategy has to change. Faced with imminent elimination, caution is no longer an option; you will have to change tack and adopt a high-risk strategy.

So how do you know your position in relation to the others? Some poker software gives you some (but not all) of the information you need in the game window.

An example from PokerStars is shown below:

Being able to see instantly how you are doing in a tournament is extremely useful. Poker software that doesn't provide this information in the game window should be avoided, particularly if you intend to play a lot of tournaments.

Here, you can see your current position in the tournament, the number of players remaining, and details of the other players' stacks – highest, lowest and average, and the level of the blinds

More detailed information on the tournament will be found in the poker room's lobby

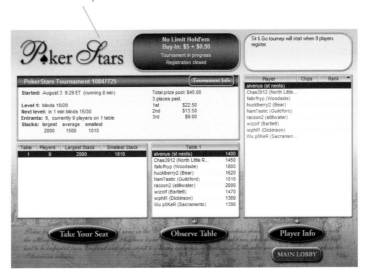

General Tournament Strategy

Essentially, tournaments come in two types (albeit with several variations). These are: a) long-handed (multi-table), and b) short-handed (single-table).

In this section, we will describe a general no-limit Texas Hold'em strategy, which holds good for both types.

Early Stages

The general rule is to play a very tight game to begin with. You don't want to be making any risky plays until you have evaluated the opposition.

Playing a very tight game initially has benefits at the later stages. Your opponents will put you down as a rock, and will continue to do so for a good while after you open up with your big guns.

In the early stages of any tournament there will be a good number of bad, impatient, and aggressive players hoping to gain an early advantage. To this end, they will be going all-in with high pairs and Ax hands. These are precisely the sort of players you want to avoid early on; let them eliminate themselves.

Play nothing but A-A, K-K, Q-Q, J-J and A-K suited; fold everything else. If you don't get any of these hands, don't worry about it. It doesn't matter too much if you don't play a single hand at this stage. Remember, all you'll be losing is a small amount in the blinds. While you are doing this, many of your opponents will be doing the opposite and getting themselves busted-out, or short-stacked.

Do not try any bluffing maneuvers early on. There will still be many bad players in the game to whom a bluff means nothing. They will simply call your bet, thus placing you in a difficult situation.

Even hands like A-K and K-Q are not worth playing. In cash games, you would bet hard on these hoping to knock-out the opposition. In the early stages of a tournament, however, several players are likely to call your bet. As a result, you may well end up trapping yourself with the second-best hand.

Having said all this, don't pass up the opportunity provided if you get A-A. With these cards you should definitely go all-in. Although it may not work, resulting in an early bust-out, remember that you are always the favorite to win in this situation. More often than not, you will win the hand and double-up. When you do, you will be in a strong position. This is how tournaments are won.

Bluffing is also something you should avoid. At this stage there will be too many players who are likely to call one.

Middle Stage

At this point, most of the maniacs and otherwise bad players will have been eliminated. The few that are left will be the ones who got lucky. The remainder will be mostly reasonable players with a sprinkling of good ones.

Now is the time to loosen up and play a still tight, but more aggressive, game. You need to start winning some pots now for two reasons: a) to keep the blinds (which are now becoming more of a threat) at bay, and b) to have a decent stack for when you reach the final table. Whereas before you were playing only the top hands, now you will be playing a greater range of hands, and playing them aggressively with good-sized bets.

Your tight play in the early stages will have convinced the opposition that you don't take risks. Also, they will now be better players who are more likely to respect a bluff. So you are now perfectly placed to try this tactic.

Short-stacked players are the obvious target here. The longer the tournament goes on, the more of a threat the blinds become to them. Use your large stack to pressurize them into making mistakes. This is the ideal situation in which to use the all-in bet. If you lose, you lose some; if they lose, they lose it all.

With the blinds at a decent level, this provides another opportunity to increase your stack by stealing them. This is where your tight table image will again be useful.

As you approach the latter stages, you need to evaluate your position. Use the software to see how you stand in relation to players at the other tables. Just because you're large-stacked at your table, doesn't mean you are large-stacked overall. If you're well below the average then you need to start taking some risks to improve your position. If your stack is at a critical level in relation to the blinds, go all-in on the first half-decent hand you get – any pair or Ax will do.

As the final table approaches, keep a close eye on the opposition. For example, if there are 15 players left and 5 of them have much lower stacks than you then play safe; they are the ones unlikely to make it. Let them fight it out between themselves.

To win a tournament, you will need to take calculated gambles. If you don't do this, while you may well hang in to the later stages, you will never reach a money-paying position.

With the blinds at a much higher level, try and steal them when you are in late position. This can be a useful way of maintaining your stack. Don't try this in the early stages of the tournament, though. You are more likely to be called by bad players, plus the size of the blinds won't be high enough.

Final Table

Depending on the size of the tournament, you will usually be in the money already. However, finishing tenth is not usually going to win you much – every position you gain now is going to increase your winnings considerably.

How you approach this final stage of the game is largely dependent on how many chips you have.

High/Medium Stack

Take no risks initially; in particular, avoid confrontations with other large-stacked players. These players tend to play either very aggressively to kill off the opposition, or very tightly in an attempt to outlast them. Don't get involved with the former unless you have a very good hand. The latter, however, are susceptible to bluffs and blind stealing. Basically, just sit tight for a while and let the opposition thin itself out.

When there are four or five players left, start playing more aggressively. You need to start winning some pots now to stay ahead of the blinds and retain "stack power". You should be looking to attack short-stacked players with large bets whenever possible. They are your target and you should always try to eliminate them before they get a chance to get back in the game (it's not uncommon for a player to be on the verge of elimination, only to make a comeback and end up winning the tournament).

If you arrive at the final table short-stacked, you may as well go for it by taking some risks. This might get you back in the game with a bit of luck. If you don't, the blinds will get you sooner or later.

Short-Stack

The advice here is to make a move while you still have enough chips to make it effective. The biggest mistake you can make in this situation is to leave it too late to try and get back in the game. If you do it early enough then a few calculated gambles and bluffs could do the trick. If you leave it too late, though, the all-in bet becomes the only option. Even if you win, the amount you win will not usually be enough as you have only a few chips left.

When you're down to your final opponent, you're in a heads-up situation. This is poker in its purist form and it is very difficult to master. An experienced heads-up player will beat an inexperienced one every time. If you intend to play a lot of tournaments, heads-up play is something you will definitely need to learn.

Playing Heads-Up

If you are going to win serious money playing tournaments, heads-up play is something you will have to master.

Start Cards

The first thing to be aware of is that you can (and must) play a much greater range of start cards. As an illustration of this, the average hand in poker is J-7 unsuited; these two cards give you a fifty/fifty chance of winning against one opponent. Anything higher makes you the favorite. This means that hands such as T-8, Q-5 and K-3, which you would fold in a normal game, are raising hands that will win more often than not. Pairs, aces, and high suited cards are monster hands in heads-up poker.

Hands that you should not play are those containing two middle or low cards, even if they are suited, connected, or both. Remember, high cards win pots at heads-up, low cards lose pots.

Style of Play

In terms of playing style, the aggressive approach is by far the best. The key to success in heads-up is winning lots of small pots rather than the occasional huge one, and you do it by keeping your opponent under constant pressure. With this type of strategy, the bluff is a very important play and helps maintain the pressure. Calling is a defensive option and, as such, is not something you should be doing much of.

Position

In heads-up poker, you are either first or last to act. If it's first, you should always bet, even with a trash hand like 7-2 off-suit. By doing so you are putting the onus on your opponent. More often than not, the other player will also have a trash hand and will fold. It won't always work and, with really trash hands, you'll have to fold if your bet is called, but at least you will be keeping the pressure on.

Stack Size

The further ahead you are, the more aggressively you should play. The more short-stacked your opponent becomes, the less inclined he or she will be to bet and thus you'll win many uncontested pots.

If you are well behind, the all-in bet is your way back into the game. Do it with any hand better than J-7.

When deciding whether to play or fold a starting hand against one opponent, a J-7 hand is a good reference. Every hand higher than this, statistically, will be the favorite to win.

To win at heads-up poker, you simply must play aggressively; it gives you a big advantage. If you allow your opponent to gain the initiative, you will be on the back foot.

Playing Single-Table Tournaments

Essentially, a STT is a quick version of a MTT, and in terms of strategy, you should play it in the same way: tight in the early stage, more loosely in the middle stage and aggressively at the end.

The blinds in a ten-seat single-table tournament are as shown below:

Level 1 – 15/30
Level 2 – 30/60
Level 3 – 50/100
Level 4 – 100/200
Level 5 – 200/400
Level 6 – 400/600
Level 7 – 600/1200
Level 8 – 1000/2000

One of the most important differences between them is that the STT will take about an hour to complete, and so everything will happen much more quickly. This means that you cannot just sit there and wait for the top hands – they might never come.

Therefore, bluffing is an essential part of these tournaments. In the space of the hour or so needed to win one, you may get only one or two really good hands and if this is the case, you are going to have to make something from lesser hands in order to survive. Observation of how your opponents play is a critical factor here; you must choose the right player(s) when making a bluff. For example, pick those who usually fold when faced by a large bet – these are the players against whom you can bluff with a marginal hand.

To break even when playing these tournaments, you need to finish third in one out of every two you play (see the prize structure on page 117). Note that this ignores the fee taken by the poker room. To win money, therefore, you need to finish at least second in one out of every two played or third in both of them. In either case, though, you won't be winning much; to do this you must win one in three.

STTs represent one of the most likely ways to win money at online poker.

Another point to be made is that playing STTs is probably the easiest (and also the least risky) way to win money at poker. There are several reasons for this:

1) With a good strategy and just nine opponents to beat, you are going to finish in the money enough times to make it profitable. This is especially so at the low buy-in tournaments where the standard of play is generally not too good.

2) Your bankroll is going to be subject to much lower variance in terms of upward and downward swings. This can be an important psychological factor in your overall game.

3) Losing streaks will make a much lower dent in your bankroll as you can lose no more than the buy-in for any given tournament.

Omaha

In this chapter you'll learn how to play Omaha with the emphasis on the Hi/Lo version of the game.

We'll cover it in the same way as we did with Texas Hold'em, explaining start card requirements and strategies for each stage of the game with the aid of sample hands.

Chapter Nine

Covers

Introduction

Next to Texas Hold'em, Omaha is the most popular version of poker. There are two variations of this game: Omaha High and Omaha Hi/Lo (also known as Omaha Eight). Both types are available in the majority of online poker rooms.

It is vital that you be aware of the fact that hands that are good in Texas Hold'em are marginal hands in Omaha.

The basic structure of Omaha is very similar to Texas Hold'em – start cards, four betting rounds, community cards, and the blinds. However, there are two major differences, which make the dynamics of Omaha completely different.

These are:

1) Players are dealt four start cards.

2) To make a hand, players must use two of their start cards and three of the community cards.

The fact that there are four start cards changes the starting hand requirements considerably. This is the first thing that Omaha beginners will have to learn. The main effect is that hand values are considerably lower than in Hold'em. With two extra cards, monster hands like full houses and quads are much more likely to be seen. Hands that are excellent in Hold'em (straights, flushes, and sets) are regularly beaten in Omaha.

With seven cards available, it is much more common for players to hit a good hand in Omaha. This in turn leads to more betting (thus, bigger pots) and general action. This makes Omaha a more exciting game than Texas Hold'em.

The requirement that a hand must consist of two of the player's start cards and three of the community cards may seem, on the face of it, to be a fairly simple concept to understand. It is, however, quite confusing initially, and takes some time to grasp. Beginners often think they have hit a good hand when, in fact, they have nothing (even pros misread Omaha hands occasionally).

Omaha Hi/Lo introduces another element: the concept of two winning hands: the highest hand winning half the pot and the lowest hand winning the other half. Sometimes, a hand is both the highest and the lowest and scoops the entire pot. This is the game that we're going to concentrate on in this chapter.

Although it's confusing initially, (especially Omaha Hi/Lo with the split pot concept), once you've got to grips with it you'll find that fixed-limit Omaha is actually a simpler and more straightforward game than Texas Hold'em.

It is also generally considered to be the easiest of the online poker games to win. There are two reasons for this:

1) Quite simply, most players are not very good at Omaha.

2) A high degree of skill is not required. The differential between good and bad players is much less than in Texas Hold'em for this reason. A good strategy, and the discipline to stick to it, will be enough to beat most online players, especially at the lower limits.

On average, a good player will win 50% more in any given hour in Omaha than in Texas Hold'em.

Most players graduate to Omaha from Texas Hold'em and, initially, assume that what was good there will also be good in Omaha. For example, they will play a pair of aces in the same way they would in Hold'em, not realizing that in Omaha this hand has little chance of winning a pot. Also, Omaha is particularly unforgiving on the two fundamental mistakes that most players make – playing bad start cards, and not knowing when to fold.

Omaha is a drawing game: players are looking to hit a five-card hand, which means a straight or higher. Pairs, two-pairs, and even sets (to a lesser degree) are not good hands at all. With four start cards, most players will be on a draw of some kind, and usually at least one or two will bet through to the river. For this reason, tactical skills, such as bluffing, check-raising, and positional play, which are so important in Texas Hold'em, lose much of their effectiveness.

Because most players concentrate on Texas Hold'em, you will find that there are fewer occupied Omaha tables. This can be restricting if you are looking for a table with weak players.

The basis of playing Omaha to win is start card selection. Remember, this game is all about hitting big five-card hands, which means drawing plenty of cards. To do this profitably, you need start cards that give you several possibilities of hitting that big hand.

Evaluating Your Start Cards

The first thing we'll look at is how to evaluate your start cards. While you have four of these, remember that you can only use *two* of them. We'll do this with some examples.

To win at Omaha, you will need very strong hands. At the minimum, you should be looking to make a straight. Even sets, which are a powerful hand in Texas Hold'em, are often beaten.

This looks like a wonderful hand; alas, it's not. Actually, it's a trash hand. All you've got is two queens. Furthermore, as the other two queens are out, there is no way to make a set, or quads. Also, you have no flush or straight draws. Fold it: you'll only lose money with this hand.

Omaha start cards should offer at least two different ways of hitting a strong hand. If they don't, they are not worth playing.

This also looks like a wonderful hand and, indeed, it is. You've got two top pairs (although you can only use one of them), a flush draw in both hearts and diamonds, two straight flush draws, plus two chances of quads and a full house.

Another example:

This is a good hand. While you don't have quad or full house possibilities, you have a flush draw in both hearts and spades, and three straight draws (8-9, 9-T, and T-J). This hand you will definitely play.

A final example:

Ideally, you should only be trying to hit hands that will be the nuts if they complete. Hitting a low straight or flush is not usually good enough.

This is another trash hand. Yes, it offers straight possibilities (3-4, 4-6), but if any of them hit, it's going to be a low-card hand. This raises an important point: Omaha is a game of nut hands, so when drawing to a straight or flush, you should be trying to make the best possible hand, e.g. an ace high flush. It's very common for two opponents each to be holding the same hand; the one with the highest card wins the pot. Many players fall into the trap of thinking they've won the pot with a good flush only to see an opponent reveal an ace high flush.

You need to be aware that while an ace is the best low card you can hold, it's not the determining factor in how good your low-hand is. It is, in fact, the least significant card. When evaluating the strength of a low-hand, you work down from the highest card.

For example: player A has 8-7-5-3-2 and player B has 8-7-5-4-A. You might think that player B has the best hand because of the ace. In fact, it's player A. Working downwards, the first three cards (8-7-5) are common to both players. The deciding cards are the fourth – player A's 3 is lower than player B's 4.

Omaha Hi/Lo introduces another variable – the split pot. Here, players have two targets – the highest hand, which takes half the pot, and the lowest hand, which takes the other half.

The lowest hand must include five cards (two from the player's hand and three from the community cards) between an ace and an eight. For example, 2-4-5-7-8. If no player manages to make a low card hand then the entire pot is won by the highest hand.

Determining the strength of a low-hand can be confusing, so we'll explain this a bit more (also, see the margin note). The best possible complete hand is A-2-3-4-5. The second best hand is A-2-3-4-6. The third best is A-2-3-4-7, and so on. The worst hand is 4-5-6-7-8.

It is also possible for a player to have both the lowest and the highest hand, and thus "scoop" the entire pot. An example would be: Ah-2h-3h-5h-6h. Here, the hand gives the nut flush for the high-hand and, also, a very good low-hand.

Ideally then, you want a hand that will be both the highest and the lowest. We'll take a look now at the start cards that you should be playing in Omaha Hi/Lo, and the ones you should be folding.

Omaha Start Cards

When your start cards are dealt, you have three things to consider:

1) Will they make a high-hand?

2) Will they make a low-hand?

3) Will they make a high-hand and, also, a low-hand?

Forget the hand values you learned in Texas Hold'em. In Omaha, the lowest hand you can bet on with any degree of confidence is a straight, and even with this you need to be wary.

High-Hand Start Cards

Here you are looking for cards that will give you as many ways to make a hand as possible. You need to remember the following:

- Pairs, and two-pairs, are not good hands in Omaha. Cards that are unlikely to make better hands than these should be folded

- A straight is often the *minimum* hand needed to win

- Your hand should contain at least one (preferably two) high suited connector(s)

The ideal high-hand will be four high cards, connected and double-suited.

The best possible hand is A-A-K-K double-suited, as shown below.

The best of the rest is any four-card combination between an ace and a ten. For example, Q-J-A-A, K-T-T-A, K-K-A-T, etc. If two of the cards are connected, so much the better; this increases the chances of a straight. If the cards are suited then you have a flush draw. These hands you will play in any position.

Playing low and middle ranked start cards is a recipe for disaster in Omaha.

Dangerous High-Hand Start Cards

Low cards, generally, should not be played. If you make a hand, it is going to be a low-card one, and you will end up being beaten more often than not.

The following are the types of hand you should not play.

- Middle and low card flush and straight draws
- Middle and low pairs
- One high pair with nothing else

To illustrate the dangers of playing these hands, we'll look at a couple of typical examples:

These cards offer several straight draws and one flush draw. Say the flop brings 8-T-J. This gives you a jack high straight, which you will no doubt consider to be a good hand. An opponent who is holding 8-9-Q-Q, though, will have a queen high straight. Your hand was good but it wasn't the nuts (or even close to it). Playing these low and middle card draws will cost you dearly.

Pairs can easily turn into sets and, as we all know, sets are a very good hand – in Texas Hold'em. But this is Omaha.

Start Cards

 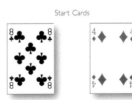

You hold two fours and, also, a low flush draw. You bet and the flop brings As-4s-9c (see next page), giving you a set, and an outside chance of a flush. All but one of your opponents fold.

You have a reasonable hand (the set), and also have a shot at a flush. Furthermore, the board doesn't look too threatening. With only one opponent to beat, you think you have a very good chance of winning. You bet and your opponent calls the bet. The turn card brings the seven of clubs, so the board is now:

Flop Cards

Turn Card

Needing one more club for your flush and with a set as a backup, you bet. Your opponent calls and the river card brings the queen of clubs giving you the flush. You bet the hand out, the showdown comes, and your opponent turns up 7s-7h-Kc-5c. The other player not only had a higher set, but also hit a higher flush.

The lesson in all this? You played a low pair that was never going to lead to a nut hand. Unfortunately, you hit a reasonable hand (the set) that enticed you to continue playing. This gave you a chance to turn the reasonable hand into a good hand (the low flush). You hit this and, on the strength of it, bet the hand out.

You trapped yourself: once you got involved with these cards, you couldn't get out. Low and middle pairs rarely result in a hand good enough to win.

Low-Hand Start Cards

Be absolutely clear on this: low-hands must contain five cards between an ace and an eight. Also, you can't use two cards of the same rank (see page 137).

As we saw on page 131, the best possible complete low-hand is five cards of consecutive rank from an ace to a five, i.e. A-2-3-4-5. The worst possible hand is 4-5-6-7-8.

Pairs, sets, straights, flushes, quads, and full houses have no relevance with regard to low-hands. All that counts is that you have five *different* ranks between an ace and an eight. Cards above eight do not qualify. This makes evaluating your start cards extremely straightforward – you need just two cards between an ace and an eight, the lower the better. The ideal hand, therefore, will contain an ace and a two. An ace and a three is not so good, an ace and a four even less so, and so on.

You also have another factor to consider. Ideally, you want to win the high-hand as well. This will enable you to scoop the entire pot, instead of just half of it. This complicates things considerably: all of a sudden, sets, straights, flushes, etc, are back in the equation.

Consider the following two examples:

As regards the low-hand, you have an ace and a four: the best card and a reasonable card. However, you have absolutely nothing with which to make a high-hand – no pairs, no straight draw, no flush draw. Compare this with the example below:

If you get confused with the examples on this page, remember the following two

rules:

1) *You can use only two of your start cards.*

2) *You can use the same two start cards for both the low-hand and the high-hand.*

Here, you have an ace and a two, which are the best possible cards for a low-hand. For the high-hand, you have a pair of aces (possible set, quads, and full house), two flush draws, and a straight draw. Furthermore, if any of these hands hit, they will be the nuts.

Let's see another type of hand:

These cards give you a chance of a good high-hand (J-J) and a good low-hand (2-3) but not both.

The table below lists the recommended start cards to play in Omaha Hi/Lo.

The table here makes it clear that you should be playing only very high cards, very low cards, or combinations of the two.

Top Hands
A-A-2-2, A-A-2-3, A-A-2-x, A-A-3-x, A-2-3-x, A-2-K-K, A-2-Q-Q, A-3-4-5, A-3-4-6, A-3-5-6, A-2-K-J, 2-3-Q-Q, 2-3-K-K, A-3-K-K, A-3-Q-Q, A-2-K-Q, A-A-K-K, A-A-Q-Q
Good Hands
A-2-x-x, 2-3-4-x, A-K-Q-J, K-Q-J-T, K-Q-J-9, A-K-Q-T, K-K-J-J, K-K-2-4, Q-J-T-9, A-A-x-x, K-K-Q-Q, A-3-x-x, K-K-T-T
A – Ace, K – King, Q – Queen, J – Jack, T – Ten, 9 to 2 – card value x – any card

The important things to remember are:

High-Hand

1) The hand must contain four cards, ten or above. This gives you a good chance of hitting a high straight at the minimum. If you play lower cards, you are going to end up hitting the second-best hand time after time.

High-hand start cards should include at least two suited cards to give the chance of a flush.

2) At least two of the cards should be suited to give the chance of a flush.

3) Hands containing four cards of the same rank, e.g. Q-Q-Q-Q must be folded, as they offer nothing better than a pair.

Low-Hand

1) The hand must contain two cards between an ace and a three. If you play cards higher than these, you will hit second-best hands far too often.

2) Suited and connected cards are important only with regard to the high-hand. They add nothing in terms of value to the low-hand.

3) If you have a pair, eight or lower, you will not be able to make a low-hand unless you have another low card of a different rank (see page 137).

Low-Hand Qualification

We have already seen that to qualify as a low-hand, the hand must contain five cards, eight or lower. This is straightforward enough to understand. However, there are two other conditions that confuse many people initially. These are:

1) Sets, straights, flushes, quads, etc, do not count towards the strength of a low-hand.

2) You can use only one card of a particular rank – paired cards don't count twice.

 Pairs, two-pairs, sets, straights, flushes, full houses, and quads only count toward the high-hand. For the low-hand, they have no relevance.

We'll explain these with a couple of examples:

Flop Cards   Turn Card   River Card

You have the ace and the four of clubs in your hand and the board shows the six, seven and eight of clubs, as shown above. Thus, you have a club flush. The flush does not count towards your low-hand, though; your low-hand is just A-4-6-7-8. An opponent holding A-3-6-7-8 with no flush would beat you. However, it does count towards your high-hand (in this case you've got the nut flush). The same applies to straights. If you have 4-5-6-7-8, an opponent holding A-2-3-7-8 will beat you for the low-hand. Your straight will count towards your high-hand, though.

Flop Cards   Turn Card   River Card

 Pairs do not count twice towards a low-hand. Remember this. Otherwise, you will think you have a qualified low-hand when, in fact, you don't.

You're holding a five and a six, and the board has three cards below nine. Thus, you may think you have a qualified low-hand – 3-3-5-6-8. Unfortunately, though, you don't. This is because you can only use a card of a particular rank once. In the example above, only one of the threes counts towards your hand. All you've actually got is 3-5-6-8, which is not a hand at all.

Pre-Flop Strategy

The strategy outlined here is based on playing the start cards recommended on page 136. If you stick to these, you will usually be drawing to nut hands, or very close to them. Thus, if you hit your hand, it will usually take the pot. And remember, because more players see the flop in Omaha, pots are usually larger than in comparable Texas Hold'em games.

As a general rule, with top hands you should not raise the pot pre-flop. If you do, you risk your opponents folding as they are going to know you have a good hand. By just calling, you won't give them any warning. This will encourage them to stay in the game.

Notice that this is completely contrary to Texas Hold'em strategy. There, you play top start cards like A-A aggressively to limit the competition because they are so vulnerable to drawing hands post-flop. In Omaha, you want the opposition to remain in the game because if you hit your hand it's going to win.

Another advantage of not raising pre-flop is that if the flop misses you completely, you can then fold without having lost too much money.

The exception to the above is if you are on the button (last to act). The opposition will have already put money in the pot, and thus will be less inclined to fold to a raise. By raising in this position only, you will build the pot, and at the same time cause fewer opponents to fold than would otherwise be the case.

If you play cards that are not likely to hit a nut hand (those in the Good Hands category in the table on page 136), then raising pre-flop to drive out some of the competition is not a bad move. Basically, you should play these hands as you would a pair of aces or kings in Texas Hold'em. Never forget: Omaha is a game of nut hands. If you don't have the best possible hand of any type, you are going to get beaten frequently unless you can limit the competition.

As a final note, be very wary of betting heavily on a low-hand if it doesn't contain an ace. At a ten-seat table, 40 cards will be dealt to the players, and five will be dealt as community cards. That leaves only seven cards not in play. If you don't have an ace, someone else almost certainly will.

Another exception to the rule of not raising pre-flop is if the best hand you are likely to make is a straight. In this case, you will need to force out the flush draws. It must be said, though, that if a straight is your best prospect, you would probably be better off folding the hand.

It can be difficult to weigh up the value of a low-hand. Try thinking of it like this: a two is the equivalent of a king, a three the equivalent of a queen, a four the equivalent of a jack, and so on.

Reading the Board

It is absolutely essential that you can read the board quickly and without making a mistake. As you can see from the examples on this page, with nine cards to look at, and the requirement that you use two of your start cards and three from the board, it isn't easy.

Before we get into post-flop strategy, there are two things that you must be clear on. The first is that you know how to read the board in relation to your start cards. Remember, you can only use three of the community cards – no more, no less, just *three*. The hand is completed by *two* of your start cards. For example:

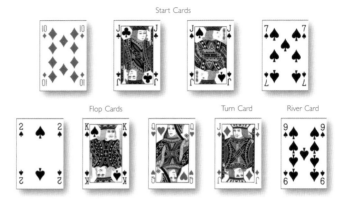

These cards give you several hands: a straight – 9-T-J-Q-K, a set of jacks, and a king high spade flush. Your best hand is the flush.

Another example:

You must have something really good here: queen quads? A full house (queens full of kings)? a king high flush? Sadly, not. A set of queens with a king kicker is the best you can muster. If these examples aren't immediately obvious to you then get a pack of cards, deal some hands and practice reading them.

Counterfeiting

The second thing you need to know about is what is meant by the term "counterfeiting" and the effect it can have on a low-hand.

Counterfeiting occurs when one of your low-hand start cards is matched by one falling on the board. The board card nullifies or "counterfeits" the card in your hand, and effectively weakens it. Whereas before you may have had the best hand, you may now find yourself holding the second-best hand.

Another way to look at counterfeiting is in high-hand terms. For example, you are holding J-T and the flop is 9-8-7 giving you the nut straight. The turn card, however, is a T. Now, an opponent holding J-Q will have a 8-9-T-J-Q straight, which beats your 7-8-9-T-J. The T falling on the turn counterfeited the T in your hand.

Consider the following example:

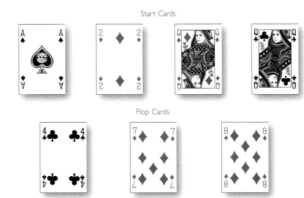

Start Cards

Flop Cards

You have a low-hand of A-2-4-7-8. However, the turn card brings another 2. Note that this doesn't change your hand: you still have A-2-4-7-8. However, an opponent holding A-3-9-9 will now have A-2-3-4-7, whereas before the turn that player's hand was A-3-4-7-8. Your hand is now beaten.

Because of the danger of having the best hand counterfeited, be very wary when a card falls on the board and matches one in your low-hand, particularly if it's an ace or a two.

Let's look at a slightly different scenario. Your start cards are A-2-3-Q, and the board cards are the same as above – 4-7-8.

In this situation, a 2 falling on the turn or river would not weaken your hand because you have a 3 as a "backup" card (known as counterfeit protection). To make your hand, you would use the A and the 3 from your start cards, and the 2, 4, and 7 from the board. You would then have the same hand as your opponent – A-2-3-4-7.

Playing the Flop

When playing the flop, you should always remember the following:

In Omaha, you should always be looking to hit a five-card hand (straights, flushes, or full houses). While two-pairs do take some pots, they don't do it often enough to make these hands worth playing.

- Pairs and two-pairs rarely win. Even sets often end up as second- or third-best hands

- Whenever there is a pair on the board, there is a strong possibility that someone has a full house

- A straight is often the minimum hand needed to win the high-hand

- You should always be looking to hit the nuts in whatever type of hand you are trying to make

- Don't bank on being able to out-play the opposition. Tactics play a lesser role in Omaha

If you bear the above in mind, your decisions will usually be correct. You won't be throwing away the money that most other players do by drawing to hands that are never going to win even if they hit them.

Whenever the board is paired, full houses become a real possibility. However, in the example here, even if the board hadn't been paired, you would still have to consider folding because of the flush possibility. At best, you would call and see what the turn card was.

We'll start with three examples of hands that you should fold.

Start Cards   Flop Cards

There is a case to be made for playing this hand. You have Q-Q and several straight draws. Furthermore, they are all high, so if you hit one it's going to be close to the nuts. However, the board is paired (J-J), and with four start cards it's almost certain that an opponent has a pair in his or her start cards, and thus is very close to a full house. Plus, there are two hearts on the board so a flush is also a very strong possibility. Even if you hit your straight, there are too many ways it can be beaten to justify the attempt.

Another example:

Start Cards · Flop Cards

When deciding whether to play a marginal hand that can win only one end of the pot, remember that even if it wins, you will only get half the money that's in the pot. Furthermore, if an opponent has the same hand, that end of the pot will be split, in which case you will get only a quarter of it. In Omaha, this is known as being "three-quartered". Very often, it won't be worth playing the hand for this reason.

You've flopped a middle straight – 6-7-8-9-T. It's also a high-end straight, and you will probably play it to the end. However, an opponent holding J-T only needs a 9 to complete a higher straight. You may think this to be unlikely, but remember: there are two cards still to come and your opponents have four start cards to choose from. It is, in fact, extremely likely.

Even so, it might be worth playing this hand it if weren't for one thing: the lack of a low-hand. You have no cards below a 9, which means you have no way to make a low-hand, and so can only win half the pot. The risk outweighs the reward. This hand you should probably fold. At best, you would call, but fold to a raise.

A final example:

Start Cards · Flop Cards

If the flop misses you completely as shown here, save your money and fold. You'll get much better opportunities.

This is a good illustration of a terrible flop. The hand started out promisingly enough – a good low-hand, a middle straight draw, a nut flush draw, and a low flush draw.

The flop, though, has bought nothing but bad cards. All you have is Q-Q with an ace kicker, and a weak middle straight draw. The flush possibilities are gone, and you can't make a low-hand. Plus, the board is paired, meaning a probable set or a full house for an opponent.

All you can do with this hand is to dump it.

Now, we'll look at some examples of hands with which you should raise.

Playing the flop in Omaha can be somewhat mechanical as everyone is trying to hit the same types of hand – straights, flushes, and full houses. Often, it comes down to seeing whose hand is closest to the nuts.

You have flopped a nut straight (T-J-Q-K-A), which is very nice. The problem, though, is that there are two hearts on the board. If either the turn or the river brings another heart then your straight is in dire danger of being trumped by a flush. If the turn and river cards are both hearts then your straight will almost certainly be beaten. Remember, the chance of a flush turning up is much greater than in Texas Hold'em.

So you raise. If the opposition all fold, you'll only win a small pot. Better that, though, than losing a big one. If they don't fold, and a heart doesn't come, you've built the pot for your straight.

Another example:

Start Cards   Flop Cards

You have an A-3-5-6-8 low-hand, which is good but not wonderful. You also have a J-J high-hand, but anyone holding an A, K or Q can beat this on the turn or river.

So you need to do two things here: limit the competition, and also find out if anyone has better cards. The only way to do this is to raise the pot. If enough of the opposition fold, it's worth paying to see the turn card. However, if you are re-raised then you are probably beaten already, and should either fold, or just call.

Playing the Turn and the River

If you've hit your hand, it should be the nuts, or very close to it (assuming you're playing the correct start cards). Play the cards in the way most likely to get your opponents' money in the pot.

If the pot is big and you have a chance to scoop it by winning both the high- and low-hands, it is usually worth paying to see the river card (see margin note below).

If you haven't, however, you need to consider how much of the pot you are likely to win if you manage to make the hand on the turn or the river. For example:

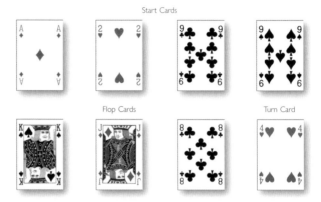

You need the river card to be a 3, 5, 6, or 7 to complete a low-hand. Your pair of nines has no chance of taking the high-hand. Unless the pot is very big, it's not worth paying another two bets to try and win half the money. Fold your hand and wait for a better opportunity.

As an illustration of why scooping the pot is so important, consider the following:

If the final pot is $100 and you have contributed $25, by winning half of it ($50) your profit is $25. However, if you scoop the entire pot ($100) your profit is $75. In the first instance you are getting even money on your bet, and in the second, you are getting odds of 3:1.

If you have one half of the pot covered with a very good hand (high or low), you should try and take the other half as well. For example:

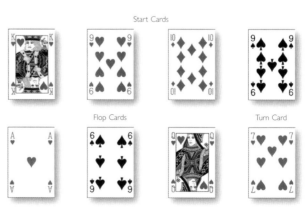

You've got the nut flush for the high-hand, but no low-hand. Most players would slow-play in this situation. However, if you raise, you may get opponents with a low-hand draw to fold. You would then win the entire pot and get a bigger pay-off than you would otherwise have done.

You should always try and take advantage of situations where there is no possibility of anyone hitting a low-hand, as described here.

Be on the look-out for situations when a low-hand is not possible, i.e. when there are two, or fewer, cards lower than a nine on the board. In this case, the high-hand scoops the pot. Because of this it's always worth raising in an attempt to bluff the opposition out of it. If it doesn't work, you've lost two bets, but if it does, you could win a substantial pot.

So, your primary objective on the turn and river is to scoop the entire pot; this is when you win money at Omaha. As it's not often that you will have the luxury of sitting there with both the best high-hand and the best low-hand, you need to force the issue by being aggressive.

Slow-playing a hand should only be done when you are absolutely certain that you cannot be beaten, and there's no realistic prospect of taking the other half of the pot by raising. For example:

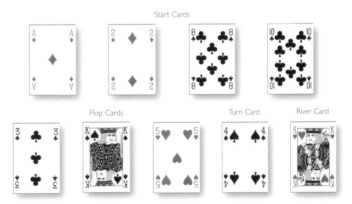

You've got the best possible low-hand, but no high-hand. With two kings on the board, you can be quite certain that someone has a set, if not a full house. You're not going to bluff anyone out of those hands by raising. So, try and maximize the pay-off from your low-hand by calling and checking to keep as many opponents in the game as possible.

Common Mistakes in Omaha Hi/Lo

If you avoid making the mistakes listed on this page, you will find it almost impossible to lose at online low-limit Omaha.

Playing Poor Start Cards

With nine cards with which to make a hand, the possibility of several good hands being hit in any one game is extremely likely. This fact makes sensible start-card selection more critical than in any other form of poker. Low-hands, in particular, should only be played if they include A-2, A-3 or 2-3.

Misreading Hands

This is a very easy (and costly) mistake to make in Omaha Hi/Lo. The requirement that: a) all hands must consist of two start cards and three board cards, and b) that low-hands must contain five cards, eight or lower, demands a high level of concentration. This is definitely not a game to play if you are tired or subject to outside distractions.

Overvaluing Hands

With the increased opportunity to hit a really good hand, hands such as high pairs, two-pairs, and sets should be played cautiously. By this we don't mean timidly (if the table conditions are right, you can play these as aggressively as any other type of hand), but rather that you be conscious of the fact that they are easily beaten.

Don't make the mistakes that many online players do by not understanding how to read the board, how low-hands are made, and how counterfeiting can ruin a good hand.

Not Taking Note of a Paired Board

Whenever the board is paired, there is a real danger of an opponent hitting either quads or a full house. In these situations, straights and flushes can be dangerous hands to be holding. If a pair falling on the board is followed by heavy betting action, folding is usually the sensible option.

Forgetting the Nuts Rule

In Omaha it is quite common to see a flush or straight beaten by a better flush or straight. Therefore, only play a drawing hand if it will be the nuts if you hit it.

Raising Pre-Flop With Top Hands

As a general rule you should do the opposite with top hands that you would in Texas Hold'em. Instead of raising to force out the competition, you should slow-play to keep as many opponents in as possible. It's at the turn and river stages that you start raising.

Seven-Card Stud

Seven-Card Stud is a very strategic game that requires a great deal of skill, much more so than Texas Hold'em and Omaha. For this reason, it is not easy to get to grips with.

Covers

Chapter Ten

Seven-Card Stud – the Rules

Before you sit down at a Seven-Card Stud table, be aware that getting to grips with this game is going to be a real challenge. You need to learn it thoroughly before you start playing for real.

Until the rise of Texas Hold'em, for many years Seven-Card Stud was the poker game of choice for most people, not only in the USA, but in many other countries, Europe in particular.

To play Seven-Card Stud successfully, you will need a high degree of skill, endless patience, good observation, and an extremely good memory. For these reasons, it is a difficult game to master.

The game is played as follows:

The Ante
Before the cards are dealt, each player places an "ante" on the table. Usually, this is equal to one quarter of the game's lower limit. For example, if the game is being played at a $1.00/2.00 table, it will be $0.25. The ante is the equivalent of the blinds in Texas Hold'em and serves the same purpose.

The Deal
First, all the antes are raked to the middle of the table. Then, beginning with the player to the left of the dealer button, each player is dealt two face-down cards and one face-up card (known as the door-card), as shown below.

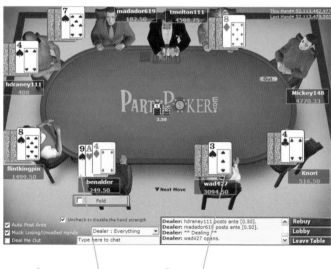

1 Your cards   2 Opponent's door card

Third Street

This is the first betting round and it is initiated by the player holding the lowest door-card. The first bet is known as the "bring-in" and is usually set at half the lower table limit. All subsequent bets in this round are at the lower limit.

Fourth Street

Each player now receives another face-up card. The second round of betting is opened by the player who has the highest face-up card. Bets in this round are, again, at the lower limit. Note that players who have a pair in their face-up cards have the option to bet at the table's higher limit. All subsequent bets and raises will also be at this level.

On Third and Fourth Street, bets are at the lower limit. From Fifth Street onwards, they are at the higher limit.

Fifth Street

When the second round of betting is complete, another face-up card is dealt to the remaining players. The player with the highest card showing now starts the third betting round. Note that bets are now at the table's higher limit and will be at this level for the rest of the game.

Sixth Street

At the completion of the third round of betting, a fourth face-up card is dealt to all the players still in the game. The fourth betting round now ensues, initiated by the player with the highest face-up card. This is shown below.

One of the differences between Seven-Card Stud and Texas Hold'em is that Stud has five betting rounds. This means that at comparable tables in terms of limits, the pot in Stud is usually higher.

Note that sometimes there are not enough cards in the deck to give each player a river card. In this case, one card is placed face-up in the center of the table where it is shared by all the players.

The River

The final stage of the game is the dealing of the river card, which is dealt face-down. All the players still in now have seven cards from which to make the best poker hand they can.

The last round of betting now takes place. If two or more players are still in at the end of it, there is a showdown (shown below). All the hands are revealed and the highest one takes the pot. In the example below, the player with the full house wins.

Factors Specific to Seven-Card Stud

Although the hands are the same as in other forms of poker, Seven-Card Stud is unique in several respects. These are:

- There are no community cards; all players have their own

- There are five rounds of betting

- It is a more expensive game to play in terms of the forced bets (the ante and the bring-in)

- Table position changes in each betting round

- Players have to base their decisions not only on their own cards, but on those of their opponents

The fact that all the cards "belong" to the players holding them (they are not shared as in Texas Hold'em and Omaha), means that if you hit a good card that improves your hand, it won't also be improving an opponent's hand. For example:

You are holding a pair of aces in Texas Hold'em with a flop of T-J-Q, and the turn card brings another ace to give you a set. However, with T-J-Q-A on the board, you would immediately be worried about the likely prospect of an opponent holding a K, and therefore having a nut straight. This type of situation doesn't arise in Seven-Card Stud. If you get a card that improves your hand, it improves your hand only.

In Seven-Card Stud, there are five rounds of betting as opposed to four in Texas Hold'em. The effect of this is that more can be won on a winning hand and more lost on a losing one. While it may be easier to improve a hand in Seven-Card Stud (as explained above), the attempt can be costly if it doesn't work.

The ante method of forcing players to contribute to the pot is more expensive than the blinds method used in other poker variants. In Seven-Card Stud, you have to stump up cash for each hand you play.

For example: playing ten hands at a $1.00/2.00 table will cost you $2.25 ($0.25 ante x 10). Plus, you have to pay the bring-in bet ($0.50). In total, you will pay out $2.75. At a same-limit ten-seat Texas Hold'em table where all the seats are taken, you will pay out $1.50 ($0.50 for the small blind, and $1.00 for the big blind) over ten hands.

Playing Seven-Card Stud costs considerably more in forced bets than Texas Hold'em or Omaha. This can add up to a significant amount over time.

In Seven-Card Stud, each betting round (apart from the first) is opened by the player who is holding the highest face-up card. This means that you never know from one round to the next where you are going to be acting from. For this reason, many players think that table position is not important and play their cards regardless. However, this is a mistake: the fact that position is not fixed in no way diminishes its importance. You just have to be flexible enough to adjust your play accordingly.

Don't make the mistake of thinking that table position is not important in Seven-Card Stud. It is just as important as in other versions of poker for the same reasons.

The most important factor of all is that there is a lot of information on the table, as so many cards are on display. Noting, remembering, and using this information is a crucial element in Seven-Card Stud. For example:

You are on Sixth Street (one more card to come) and you are holding four hearts – one more gives you a flush. If you have been taking note of the number of hearts in the face-up cards, you will now have a very good idea of how many hearts are left in the pack (live cards). If there are not many, the chances of making your flush are low, so you fold, and vice versa.

Knowing which cards are live and which aren't is also an extremely important factor in calculating the pot odds. If you don't have this information because you haven't been paying attention or have forgotten, it will be impossible to calculate them correctly.

So you can see that observation, not just of the opposition but of the cards, is a much more critical factor than it is in Texas Hold'em or Omaha.

Start Cards

Like most versions of poker, Seven-Card Stud is a game of high cards – the higher the better. The following table lists the start cards that should be played:

A good rule of thumb is only to play start cards that are all higher than the highest up-card on the table. This increases considerably the chances of you hitting the highest pair or two-pair.

Top Hands
All sets: A-A-A to 2-2-2. The higher the better Pairs: A-A, K-K, Q-Q, J-J Suited connectors: A-K-Q, K-Q-J
Strong Hands
Pairs: T-T, 9-9, 8-8 Suited connectors: Q-J-T, J-T-9 Unsuited connectors: A-K-Q, K-Q-J Gapped suited connectors: A-K-J, A-Q-J
Good Hands
High three-card flush draws: e.g. Ks-7s-4s Suited connectors: T-9-8, 9-8-7, 8-7-6 Unsuited connectors: Q-J-T, J-T-9, T-9-8 Gapped suited connectors: K-Q-T, Q-J-9 Pairs: 7-7, 6-6, 5-5
Marginal Hands
Middle & low three-card flush draws: e.g. 9c-6c-2c Pairs: 4-4, 3-3, 2-2 Suited connectors: 7-6-5, 6-5-4, 5-4-3, 4-3-2 Unsuited connectors: 9-8-7, 8-7-6, 7-6-5 Gapped suited connectors: J-T-8, T-9-7 Two high cards: e.g. A-J-5, K-J-8

From the table, you can see that good start cards are those that either form a complete hand (sets and high pairs) or give you both straight and flush possibilities.

However, it's not just a case of what your start cards are. Unlike Texas Hold'em, where pre-flop you have no idea what your opponents are holding, in Seven-Card Stud you can see one of their cards (the door-card) right from the off. This is an important factor when deciding whether to play a hand (and how to play it).

Playing Pairs

Many hands are won in Seven-Card Stud with high pairs and two-pairs. With seven cards from which to make a hand, hand values are the same as in Texas Hold'em.

High Pairs

You are holding a high pair (A-A to J-J) and your opponents' up-cards are all lower. You play this as you would in Texas Hold'em by raising to knock out opponents with drawing hands.

How about a situation where the pot has been raised and re-raised by players with higher up-cards than your pair? For example, you hold a pair of nines, and an opponent showing a ten raises only to be re-raised by one showing a queen. You can be fairly certain here that your nines are beaten, so save your money and fold.

If you're holding a pair and the other two cards of the pair are showing in your opponents' up-cards, fold. The exception to this would be if you also had a good flush or straight draw.

The exception would be if your cards were connected, or were all of the same suit. In this case, you would have the added options of a flush or straight draw, so it would be correct to call the raise and see what the next card brought. If the hand didn't improve then you would fold it.

Medium and Low Pairs

When you hold a medium pair and there are no up-cards higher than your pair on the board, you should always raise with it, assuming the pot hasn't already been raised. This is particularly so if your pair is concealed and you have a high up-card, a king for example. The opposition will immediately put you on a pair of kings, and may well fold.

Having a high up-card (A or K) provides an opportunity to bluff. A raise in this situation will make the opposition suspect that you have a matching card in your down-cards.

If the pot is raised and you have a high kicker, you should call. If the pot has been raised and re-raised, you should generally fold.

If there are up-cards higher than your pair, play it as a drawing hand. In this case, you are looking to hit a set. You don't want to be paying dearly for this, though. The chances of hitting your set are not good enough to justify calling raises. If there is heavy betting action, fold. In any case, if you haven't hit your set by Fifth Street where the bets double, you should fold anyway.

You also need to consider the opposition when deciding whether to play medium and low pairs. If you have only two or three opponents, or they're loose players, catching another card to give a two-pair will usually be good enough to win the pot.

Playing Sets

As in Texas Hold'em, sets should usually be played aggressively to force out opponents holding drawing hands.

Statistically, you will be dealt a set once in every 425 hands. The instinctive reaction of most players is to slow-play them, but usually they are making a mistake in doing so.

You must remember that there are four hands that beat a set, so being dealt one is by no means a guarantee that you are going to win. There is always a risk of an opponent hitting a higher hand, so unless you're a gambler and like taking chances, you have to raise to try and knock out players with a drawing hand.

Seven-Card Stud can produce a situation, though, when it is correct to slow-play a set, and an example of this is shown below:

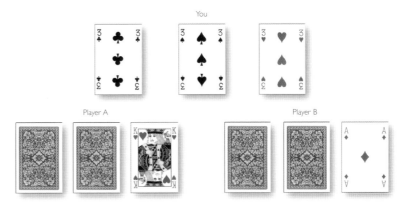

Here, you are holding a set of threes, Player A has a king up-card and Player B has an ace up-card. Everyone else has folded.

We saw on the previous page how up-cards can be used as a bluff. The example here shows how they can work against you by compelling you to make a less than optimum play.

Player A raises with the king and is immediately re-raised by Player B. Fairly obviously, one if not both of them have a top pair. Now it's your turn to act. If you re-raise Player B, they're both going to be looking at your up-card and thinking "Well, this player is not re-raising an ace with a pair of threes, so he or she must have three of them". By making this play, you've told them literally what you have, and if they are good players, they may well fold. You don't want this because against just two opponents, the set is favorite to win – you need to keep them in the game.

So the only thing that you can do is to slow-play the hand initially, and then raise on Fifth Street when the bets double. By this time, there will be a good-sized pot. This is a risky play, though, because you are giving the opposition an opportunity to hit a better hand.

Playing Drawing Hands

Cards that offer just one way of hitting a hand should be played only if the pot is likely to be big, i.e. several opponents need to be in the game. So these hands must be played from late position, which will enable you to see how many players are in.

Dead Cards

An important consideration when playing drawing hands is the number of "dead" cards. These are cards needed to complete the hand but that are held by opponents. For example:

You are dealt three spades giving you a flush draw. The pack contains thirteen of each suit, so with three already out, there are ten left. If three of your opponents have a spade up-card each, that leaves seven "live" spades. There are also fourteen other dealt cards (opponents' down-cards) and, statistically, there will be another three or four spades amongst these. So, in total, there will be nine to ten dead spades. That leaves three or four live ones with which to complete your hand. Trying to make the flush in these circumstances is simply throwing away your money.

Another important consideration is the face value of the cards. Remember, in Seven-Card Stud more pots are won by pairs and two-pairs than by straights, flushes, and other big hands. So if you start with a straight or flush draw, it should have two high cards (A to T), or at least one card that is higher than any of your opponents' up-cards. If it doesn't, you should fold. You need to have another way of making a hand in case the draw misses.

It is essential that you count (and remember) the number of dead cards. By doing this, you will always have a good idea of how likely you are to hit your hand. This information can save you countless bets drawing to cards that will never come.

Assuming the cards are good enough to play, the first thing you do is count the dead cards. If there are three or more, fold. If there are two or fewer then you can play the hand, and you should do this in much the same way as you would in Texas Hold'em.

Call any single bets in the first round, but fold to a raise; you don't want to pay any more than is necessary to see the next card. If the hand doesn't improve on Fourth Street (another card for your straight or flush, or a high pair), fold. If it does, and there are still two or fewer dead cards, continue playing.

If you still need two cards to complete the drawing hand at Fifth Street, or the dead card count has risen to three or more, you should abandon the attempt as the bets double at this stage. Now, you will play the hand on the strength of whatever pair you have.

If you need just one more card to complete the straight or flush after Fifth Street, the decision on whether to continue is based on the pot odds.

Improving Your Game

This chapter shows you some ways to improve the way you play poker – something you should always be striving to do.

Think of it in these terms: the better you become, the more money you will win. What better incentive could there be?

Covers

Practice, Practice, Practice

The most important prerequisite for becoming a successful poker player is experience. There is absolutely no substitute for this. Books will point you in the right direction but you actually need to play the game to put the theories you learn into practice.

The only way to become really proficient at something is to work at it – everybody knows this but few have the willpower and self-discipline to actually do it.

Poker is no different. The great players didn't become great overnight. Years of hard work (studying and analyzing the game), constant traveling, late nights, etc, lie behind their success.

As an online player, you have it much easier. The main thing you need to become a winning poker player – experience – is literally at your fingertips. All you have to do is log on to your favored poker room and play for as long as is necessary to understand the strategies explained in books such as this one, and develop the discipline to apply them. Furthermore, by sticking to the micro-limit tables, if, initially, you lose, the losses will be negligible.

All poker rooms provide play-money tables and many poker books suggest that these are the ideal place to learn the game without any financial risk. We disagree, for two reasons:

1) Poker *is* a game of financial risk, and if your mistakes aren't costing you hard cash, you are likely to keep on making them.

2) Because there is no real money involved, players at these tables make the most ridiculous moves – ones that would quickly bankrupt them if they tried them at a real money table. An essential part of poker is learning how to read your opponents and how to handle the various styles of play (tight, aggressive, passive, etc). At play-money tables, all you will encounter is the maniac. In short, you will learn very little that's useful. In fact, you are more likely to pick up bad poker habits, such as playing incorrect start cards, that will cost you dearly when you start playing for real. The only thing we can find in their favor is that they do allow you to get the hang of the software and develop a feel for the mechanics of the online game.

We recommend that you give the play-money tables a miss. You'll learn very little from them, and may, in fact, come away with some dangerous misconceptions.

Once you've done this, though, move on to the low- or micro-limit tables and get your practice in there.

Poker Simulation Software

You will find that there are a number of computer programs that let you practice your game on the PC. Probably the best one is from Wilson Software. This company provides a program for each of the main poker games found in online casinos – Texas Hold'em, Omaha, and Seven-Card Stud.

One of the big advantages offered by poker simulation software is that you can play a proper game of poker without the maniacs you would find at the free-money tables. Thus, the game will be much more "true to life" and you will learn more from it.

We'll take a brief look at their "Turbo Texas Hold'em" program.

The key thing with this is that the program can be configured to accurately create any table condition that you will find in the real world. For example:

- The number of players
- The "tightness" or "looseness" of play
- Parameters such as the rake, the blinds, and table limits

The set-up window is shown below:

Further advantages are that you can play as much as you like without losing a cent. Also, these programs all offer tips on how to play each hand, and tell you the odds against making them.

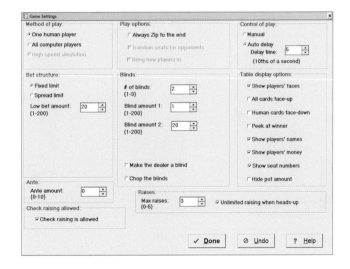

If you find yourself struggling against loose players, you can construct a table full of them. If you want to learn how to play against tight players, or a combination of loose and tight, as found in many low-limit tables, this can be set up as well.

Want to practice playing heads-up? Just select one player.

Texas Turbo Hold'em can be downloaded from www. wilsonsoftware. com. At this site, you will find similar programs for Seven-Card Stud, Omaha, and Tournament Texas Hold'em.

Click Advice, and you will be told the best way to play the hand (bet, raise, check, or fold.). Click Odds, and you will be told the exact odds against making any hand that's possible with your cards. You will also be told the pot odds (this is one of the program's most useful features and beginners should refer to it constantly)

Another poker simulation program that has a very good reputation is Poker Academy, available at www. poki-poker.com.

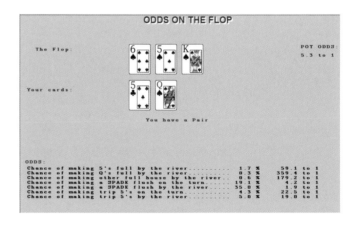

This is an excellent program and is highly recommended. Note that many professional players use Turbo Texas Hold'em to run simulations covering thousands of hands. The data is analyzed to improve their game.

Keeping Records

Players who lose consistently will find a record of their sessions to be a great aid in establishing where they are going wrong.

Government departments are addicted to records and statistics – they love them. These endless lists of data tell them all sorts of useful things – trends, patterns, opinions, etc. Businesses use them as well to see who's buying what, where they're buying, when they're buying, and so on. It enables them to spot problem areas, new opportunities, and generally get a handle on how to improve sales, and stem losses.

As a poker player, you are also in business, and if government and multi-national companies feel the need to keep records, so should you. Your poker records should include:

- The date and start/end time of each session
- The amount you win or lose
- The poker rooms in which you play
- The games you play
- The table limits
- Notes on good and bad players you encounter
- Mistakes you make

Some countries require players to keep a record of their gambling activities for tax purposes. For example, the American Internal Revenue Service requires the following details:

- *The date, and type, of your specific wager or wagering activity*

- *The amount(s) you won or lost*

- *The name and address, or location, of the gaming establishment*

The most important thing that this will do is to force you to confront reality in the event that you are losing consistently. It will be there in black and white – the amount of money you've lost (many players quickly lose track of how much they are losing and would be horrified if they knew exactly how much).

By referring to your records, you will be able to see exactly when the money is being lost, where it is being lost, and to whom it is being lost. For example, you may notice that you are losing large amounts at a specific site, which perhaps indicates that the players at this site are hard to beat. You may do better at a different site. Or it might be that you are winning at lower-limit tables and losing at higher ones. Your results may be better at Omaha than they are at Texas Hold'em. You may win more in short sessions.

By keeping a detailed record of your poker sessions, all this information will be available, and you will find it to be extremely useful.

You might not be surprised to know that you can also keep your poker records online. (Is there anything you can't do online these days?)

One such site is PokerCharts at www.pokercharts.com. This is a subscription-based service that allows you to enter details of all your poker sessions by means of various filters, and then get a graphic (line plots, bar graphs, pie charts and combination graphs) and text read-out of relevant statistics.

By keeping your records online, you will never lose them.

Statistics given include:

- Total winnings
- Overall win rate per hour
- Average win rate per hour
- Sessions played
- Games played
- Hours played
- Games you are most successful and least successful in
- The poker rooms you do best and worst in

You can also get record-keeping software. A good example of this is Poker Journal, which you can download from the Internet.

Note that PokerCharts (and similar sites) does not provide detailed analysis of poker room hand histories (for this you need hand analysis software – see page 163). It provides long-term, session-by-session analysis that, basically, gives you the "overall picture" on how well you are doing.

Obviously, you can do all this yourself but calculating the required statistics can be a time-consuming procedure. Sites like PokerCharts make it a lot easier by doing the number-crunching for you. All you have to do is spend a few minutes entering the relevant data and let the site do the rest.

At the time of writing, the service cost $11.95 for six months, $7.95 for three months, or $2.65 for one month. A free 30-day trial period is available.

PokerCharts is the original site of its type and is highly recommended.

Analyzing Your Game

We saw on page 161 how keeping a record of your sessions can help you to identify general problem areas. Poker analysis software takes this to another level by pin-pointing specific weaknesses in the way you play the hands.

Most players who lose at poker attribute their losses to bad luck. On any given day this may be true but over the long term, luck will have little to do with it. They're losing consistently because they are consistently making mistakes.

The only way to discover what these mistakes are is to analyze your game, and to do this you need statistical data on your poker sessions. This will be a detailed record of every hand you play. Fortunately, most sites provide players with this information in the form of hand histories, which can be downloaded to the PC.

The problem is making sense of it all. Over a typical three-hour online session, you will have played between 150 and 200 hands of poker. That's an awful lot of data to wade through. Once again, computer software comes to the rescue. These programs take the hand history data, assimilate it, and in a matter of seconds, present you with all the relevant statistics.

There are quite a few hand analysis programs but the most well-known one is Poker Tracker. The information provided by this program is awesome and is, quite simply, everything you could possibly need.

One problem with Poker Tracker is that it provides so much information that, initially, it can be quite intimidating. At first glance, much of the data will be meaningless. To be able to understand and make use of it you will have to spend some time reading the program's help files. It will be well worth doing, though.

The following is just some of the data Poker Tracker will provide:

- How many times you raise, call, check and fold. Also, where you make these actions (pre-flop, flop, river, etc)

- How much you win and lose in each table position

- How many times you hit each type of hand (flush, straight, etc) and how much you win and lose with them

- Every player you have played against, plus details of their actions. It also tells you which players you have won the most from and the ones who have won the most from you

- A detailed analysis of each session, or tournament, that you play

One of the program's most useful features allows you to select specific hands and play them back graphically to see what you did right or wrong. This is an absolutely wonderful aid that helps identify the types of hand that you play incorrectly and why you do so

Poker Tracker will replay any hand for you, as shown opposite. This works in the same way as a movie player, i.e. it provides playback controls, such as play and pause. This allows you to see exactly where you went wrong in the hand, so that next time, you won't make the mistake again.

You can also replay entire sessions and tournaments.

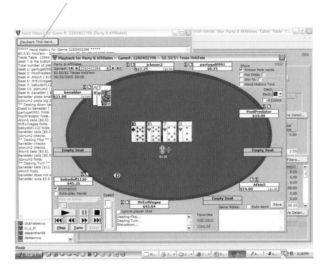

Poker Tracker also gives you a detailed analysis of the start cards you play. For example, it shows you each hand you've played, the number of times you've played them, and the number of times each one has won (this can be a real eye-opener)

We've explained the importance of taking the pot odds into account when deciding whether to play certain hands. The hand playback feature in Poker Tracker provides an ideal way to get the hang of this, as you can pause it while you calculate the odds in a real-life situation.

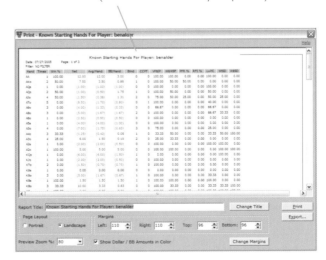

Some Other Strategies

We've told you everything you need to know to succeed at the online game. You've learned the rules of the various games, good basic strategy, the common mistakes players make, and more advanced tactics, such as the check-raise. Now, we'll show you a couple of other simple tricks.

Skipping Tables

The drawback with moving from table to table is that you lose your own "read" on the opposition.

It should be fairly obvious by now that a predictable style of play is never going to succeed. It doesn't take long for the opposition to "work you out". The way to avoid this is to vary your playing style. Some players don't like to do this, though; they have their own style and prefer to stick to it. Others find it difficult to do.

However, as an online player, you have another way to avoid being predictable. Online poker rooms provide a huge number of tables, so there is never any reason to restrict yourself to playing at the same one continuously. Take advantage of this by never staying at any one table long enough for the opposition to be able to figure you out. Play a few hands and then move on to another one.

Playing Multiple Tables

If you play poker correctly, you will be folding the majority of your start cards and simply waiting for the top pairs and high suited connectors. The problem with this is that it becomes extremely tedious after a while, and the danger is that, as a result, you start playing hands that you shouldn't because you want some "action".

Some poker software allow you to minimize the game window so that you can have up to four in full view simultaneously. This makes playing several tables much easier. Examples of sites providing this feature are Ladbrokes and UltimateBet.

Virtually all poker rooms allow players to play at several tables simultaneously, usually three or four. This provides a way to get many more hands that are worth playing in any given period. For example, if you play at three tables, you are going to get A-A three times as often as you would at just one table. With much more action, you are not going to get bored, and so will be more likely to stick to playing only good hands.

Note that we don't recommend this for complete beginners as it can be confusing to have to keep switching from one game window to another. Also, you'll often have much less time to make your decisions. And there is the danger of clicking the wrong action button, which can be a costly mistake.

How to Avoid Going On Tilt

A player who is on tilt is, quite simply, one who has lost the plot completely, and instead of playing good solid poker, plays trash hands, bets when one should be folding, and folds when one should be betting. Basically, a player on tilt gets everything wrong. The problem is compounded if the other players recognize one who is on tilt, as they will take ruthless advantage. This is the worst thing that can happen to a poker player. Those who keep on playing in this state will lose big-time. All the good work put in over a period of hours can be undone in minutes.

It is absolutely essential that you are aware of this issue and know how to avoid it. This means understanding *why* it happens, and the rather simplistic answer is that it's always down to negative emotions. It could be anger, frustration, impatience, or even just simple boredom; it really doesn't matter which. The key, therefore, is to try to avoid any situation that is likely to trigger a negative emotional response. The two most common ones are:

The Bad-Beat

Unfortunately, this is something that cannot be avoided – it happens to all players. This is what you have to remember in this situation: it was bad luck. Forget it and move on. Play the next few hands conservatively until the memory has faded. Do not try and win it back immediately as so many do.

Lack of Progress

You've been playing for hours and your stack keeps going up and down. You never get far enough ahead to be able to say to yourself "That's a nice profit for the day, I'll stop now". Eventually, you become frustrated and start playing loosely. As you start to lose as a result, you play worse. This is an insidious form of on-tilt, as it is so gradual you're not aware that it's happening. The result, nevertheless, is just as deadly.

The answer is to call a halt to the proceedings before the process begins. This is where you have to know yourself: only you know your emotional thresholds. If you're the type who gets frustrated quickly, set yourself an appropriate session period, say two hours. If you're not getting anywhere, stop playing after the two hours is up and take a break. Then have another go a bit later on.

Chapter Twelve

Miscellaneous Topics

Here we cover a range of poker-related topics. These include two very important issues: how to manage your bankroll and how to cope with losing streaks (something that happens to everyone). You will also find some recommended reading material that will help you to improve your game.

Covers

Even More Poker Games

The games mentioned on this page are only available at UltimateBet and ParadisePoker, of the leading poker sites.

Crazy Pineapple

Crazy Pineapple is yet another variation of Texas Hold'em. While the rules and the betting structure are basically the same, there are two important differences.

1) Players are dealt *three* start cards.

2) Following the second round of betting after the three flop cards are dealt, each player has to discard one of their start cards.

This can result in some interesting situations. For example, say your start cards are 8-8-J and the flop brings 10-9-8. You have a set and, also, a nice outside straight draw. But, because you have to discard one of your three start cards, you have to choose which hand to play.

In all other respects, the game is the same as Texas Hold'em.

Lowball

Lowball is basically Five-Card Draw poker with the difference that players are aiming to make the lowest hand – 1-2-3-4-5. It is also common for a joker to be included in the pack and this can be used as a wild-card.

Players are dealt five cards face-down after which a round of betting takes place. All bets at this stage are at the lower limit. When this is finished all players can discard (burn) as many of their cards as they like and replace them with new ones. The second round of betting now ensues at the higher limit. Any players left in at the end of this reveal their cards in the showdown.

Razz

This is a version of Seven-Card Stud in which the lowest hand wins. The player with the highest card is required to make the bring-in bet on the first round of betting, and the player with the lowest hand acts first on all other rounds.

The best possible hand is A-2-3-4-5 (straights and flushes do not count). Also, unlike in Seven-Card Stud, players who have a pair showing in the up-cards cannot bet at the higher limit.

PokerBots

There is a well known pokerbot (which shall remain nameless) that actually enables two or more players to collude by sharing information on a separate network. This is blatant cheating and players caught using this have their accounts closed immediately by the poker rooms.

You won't be long into your online poker career before the thorny subject of pokerbots rears its head, so we'll tell you about it now.

A pokerbot is a software program that can play poker. Nothing startling there, you may be thinking; programs exist for all popular games. Pokerbots, however, play poker for real. These programs hook into a poker room's software and operate from within a separate window on the player's PC.

The pokerbot can see all the face-up cards on the table and is programmed to make recommendations to the player as to the best course of action (bet, raise, fold, etc). It will advise on which start cards to play, and post-flop, it will work out the pot odds automatically and display them. Some pokerbots go a step further and actually play the hand without any input from the player, who only has to sit back and watch.

The two questions everyone asks is: a) are they any good?, and b) are they legal?

Some pokerbots can be programmed by the owner to play in a particular way. For example, the user may specify that the pokerbot always raises with A-A and K-K, or always folds low pairs.

It is possible to write any number of programs to suit different table conditions, and save them. These can then be loaded into the pokerbot as and when required. All that's needed is basic programming knowledge.

We'll answer the second question first. Yes, they are legal. While most of the poker rooms try to discourage players from using them, they cannot prevent them from doing so.

As regards their effectiveness, it must be said that many of them are utterly useless. There are a few, though, that are actually quite good within their inherent limitations, particularly pre-flop where they play only the correct start cards. However, as they are not "intelligent" they are unable to react to subtle moves such as the check-raise. At the lower limits, the good ones can hold their own, and maybe even show a small profit, but good players will have no problem beating them. You also have to ask yourself what is the point. They'll never make you rich, and while you're using them you won't be developing your own game.

Do other players use pokerbots? Without a doubt. Online poker players will do anything to give themselves an edge. Should the prospect of playing against a pokerbot worry you? Absolutely not. Firstly, the likelihood is slight, and secondly, you would have to be a very poor player to be beaten by the majority of them.

As a recommendation then, we suggest you give pokerbots a miss.

Bankroll Management

How to manage your money is a much overlooked aspect of the game. Successful poker is about far more than just sitting down at a table with x amount of money and playing until you've either lost it all, or simply had enough. Unfortunately, this is the approach most people take.

When you play poker regularly, there are going to be periods when you lose consistently; this is a simple and unavoidable fact of life in the poker world. Your bankroll has to be large enough to absorb these losses, and still leave you enough to let you play without having to be looking constantly at how much you have left. When you start doing this it will affect the way you play. What you do not want to be doing is reloading your account with $50, or whatever, every few hours; this can become a dangerous habit. Get a good sum of money in the account, put the credit card back in the drawer, and leave it there.

Even casinos with their built-in advantage run the risk of going broke if they don't have adequate cash reserves to sustain the inevitable ups and downs. You are no different.

The size of the bankroll needed depends on the limits at which you intend playing. We suggest a figure 200 times the higher limit. For example, at the $1.00/2.00 tables, you should have no less than $400 available. This will cover the inevitable ups and downs.

The next thing you must do is set the maximum amount you are prepared to lose in any one day, or session. If your bankroll is $1000 and you've set a daily limit of $100, $100 is what you put down on the table. When it's gone, you're gone. It is absolutely essential that you have the discipline to do this because there are going to be days when, no matter how well you play, bad luck is going to beat you.

How you handle your winnings is equally important. You may be sailing along nicely having increased your $100 stack to, say, $300, and then, all of a sudden, you start losing and the $300 disappears. When it does, not only have you lost your winnings, you have also lost your initial stack.

To prevent this happening, you should bank any significant winnings as you go. Using the example above, you could bank $150, lose your initial $100, and still end up $50 ahead of the game.

If you know that you have the discipline to stop when the $100 is gone, you will be able to play safe in the knowledge that, whatever happens thereafter in the session, you are going to finish a winner.

Bank significant winnings as you go. If you have the discipline to stop when your starting stack has gone, you should still finish the session ahead.

If you leave your winnings on the table, it will be very difficult not to play with them when the cards turn against you, and you will often end up losing them all.

If you find yourself losing over several sessions, say $200-$300 out of your $1000 bankroll, then it's time to move down to a lower limit. Always try and keep an account balance of at least 200 times the table limit. If you keep on losing, keep dropping down through the limits until you find a level at which you stop losing. Having done so, you either stick at this limit, or you learn how to improve your game so that you can start moving back up the limits.

This isn't playing poker; this is managing your money so that you don't do what most players do and run out of it. When they do, they dig the credit card out again, deposit more money, lose it, deposit more money, and so on. This road leads to the bankruptcy courts.

It is also a fact that a player can become so numbed by constant losses that succeeding losses cease to hurt. Don't fall into this trap yourself.

It's all avoidable, and good money management is the key. If you get this aspect of your game right, you should *never* lose your entire bankroll.

Good money management will also give you confidence. If the fear of going broke isn't always niggling away in your subconscious, you'll be a better player for it.

While we're not saying that bankroll management is the be-all and end-all (you do need to be a good player as well), it is important, and it's something that you will neglect at your own risk.

Handling Winning and Losing Streaks

Everyone who plays poker will experience periods when they can do no wrong and periods when absolutely nothing goes right. This happens to the best and worst of players – no one is immune.

Winning Streaks

Beware of falling into the trap of thinking you are a good player, when in reality you are a lucky one. A good player will always be a good player. This is not the case with lucky players, though – their luck will run out.

"What's there to think about here?" you may ask. "If I'm winning, where's the problem?" The answer is that while there is no immediate problem, there are two potential problems.

The first concerns *why* you are winning. If it is due to sheer luck rather than skillful play, then your winning streak is unlikely to last long. When it ends, all of a sudden those wonderful hands that were coming one after the other, and winning you pot after pot, will quickly become a distant memory. Now you won't be able to hit a pair, never mind a flush. What few good hands you do get will invariably be beaten by a better hand.

The point we are making here is that confusing good fortune for good play is a big mistake. By all means ride your luck, but be aware that if you can only win when the cards are falling for you, you are destined to be a loser in the long term.

The second potential problem is that of over-confidence. When everything is going right for you, it is very easy to fall into the trap of thinking everything will continue going right. I'll give you a good example of this. Not long ago I was in the middle of a really hot streak and was winning every other hand. I was pulling flushes, straights, and sets almost at will. There was a fish at the table who was taking a real beating from me. In spite of all the evidence on the board, this guy kept raising and re-raising me and losing every time. I was even beginning to wonder if his software was faulty and only his raise button was working.

I beat him again with a full house and the very next hand hit a set of aces. Everyone else folded but not the fish – once again he steamed in with a raise. I just couldn't believe how stupid this guy was. Then came the showdown, and to my disgust he turned up a straight with the last card coming on the river. He had caught a lucky card right at the end.

In my over-confidence I hadn't even looked at the board cards – if I had, I'd have seen the danger immediately. With a set of aces, and the fish as an opponent, I'd just assumed I was going to win. While I was still well up, this pot cost me a lot of money, and the loss was totally avoidable – all because of being over-confident.

So, take advantage of good fortune but don't let it blind you to reality, and never let yourself become so confident that you start playing carelessly.

Losing Streaks

How you handle the inevitable losing streak is probably as important as having a high level of skill. It's easy to win when the cards are falling for you, but it's not so easy to keep the money when they are against you.

The only thing you can do in this situation is minimize your losses as far as possible by just sitting tight until things improve. Simply fold every single hand until the cards improve. Alternatively, drop down to a micro-limit table where you can lose only a few dollars, and play out the losing streak there.

Unfortunately, most players do the opposite. Instead of playing fewer hands, or none at all, they play even more in an attempt to get their losses back quickly. This has a compound effect that results in them losing even more, and at a faster rate. As their losses mount, they become increasingly desperate and start taking absurd risks.

The other thing that often happens is players deciding to play at a high-limit table, reasoning that with a bit of luck, they'll get their money back quickly. Even worse, they'll take their chances at a no-limit table. Unfortunately, nothing will change – playing a high- or no-limit table will not improve their luck. They'll just go bankrupt even more quickly. This is something that you must not do.

You also need to be aware that the other players will see what is happening. If they notice you losing hand after hand, and your stack dwindling rapidly, they are going to fancy their chances against you. Every time you make a bet, they will pressurize you by raising. So deny them the opportunity by simply folding all your hands until your luck improves.

*If you are suffering heavy losses, you **must** stop playing. Take the dog for a long walk and think about what's happening. Go back 30 minutes later and you'll find yourself playing much more sensibly.*

Never, ever, move to a no-limit table in an attempt to recoup your losses quickly. While you can get lucky and win it all back in one or two good hands, remember why you're in this situation in the first place – the cards are not falling for you. If your luck's out, a no-limit table is the last place you want to be.

How Much Can You Win?

A well known saying in poker is that it's a hard way to win easy money. What this basically means is that while it's not difficult to win money once you've acquired the necessary skills, it's not so easy to win worthwhile amounts.

The first thing you want to do is forget everything you've seen on television regarding poker. Here, you will see players winning and losing thousands of dollars on a single hand. While it's real enough, it's very far from being typical. Many thousands of people have been attracted to online poker after watching the televised poker events, no doubt thinking that there's no reason they can't do the same themselves.

As a very rough guide, playing a $1.00/2.00 online table for eight hours over several days should result in average winnings in the region of $50-60 per day. Don't expect to achieve this every day, though. Some days you'll lose $50, and other days you'll win $100.

If you're thinking along the same lines, or have visions of giving up the day-job, consider this: a typical poker professional playing fixed-limit Texas Hold'em in a bricks and mortar poker room expects to win approximately one big bet an hour (a big bet is defined as the bigger of the two table limits. For example, at a $10/20 table, it will be $20). To be clear: such a player doesn't expect to win this sum *every* hour, but to *average* it. There'll be ups and downs, but overall, it will be a consistent win rate.

The average online player (who's not a professional) can expect to have a lower win rate. However, this is counterbalanced by two factors: a) at least twice as many hands are dealt in an online game in any given period, and b) the standard of the opposition is generally much lower. So assuming you are good enough, at the low-limit tables you should be able to win an average of three or four big bets an hour. The higher up the limits you go, though, the lower this figure will be.

The important thing to take from this is that you should keep your expectations at a realistic level. Poker is not going to make you rich overnight. Most players simply have no idea of what constitutes a successful poker session and will often ruin a good one by playing on long after they should have stopped.

If you want to win serious money playing poker, you have to play at the high-limit tables. This is something you must build up to, though. Start at the lower limits, and when you can beat them consistently, move up to the next limit, and so on.

The World Series of Poker (WSOP)

This is the richest and most prestigious poker tournament in the world. Held annually at Binion's Horseshoe casino in Las Vegas, (see top margin note), it represents the Holy Grail for all serious poker players.

The 2005 WSOP was held at the Rio-All Suite Hotel and Casino in Las Vegas, with the exception of the final two days of the main event. This was held at Binion's Horseshoe Casino. This is the first time that the entire event hasn't been hosted at Binion's.

The World Series of Poker began in 1971 and in that year the championship winner took home $30,000. In 1991, the prize money hit $1,000,000, and since then has continued to rocket.

The event is actually a series of tournaments covering all the main poker games, such as Texas Hold'em, Omaha, Stud, and the various versions, such as Razz and Lowball.

Buy-ins, typically, range from $1,000 to $5,000, but for the main event – the championship tournament – the buy-in is $10,000. The game in this event is Texas Hold'em, and in 2005 there were 5600 entrants for this one event alone. When you consider that the 2004 event attracted 2500 entrants, you can see how popular it is becoming.

One of the great things about the WSOP is that it is possible to reach the finals without having to put up the huge entry fees. Both the 2003 and 2004 winners qualified via low buy-in satellite tournaments. In fact, four of the players at the final table of the 2004 main event qualified via the PokerStars online poker room. In the 2005 event, again, four of the finalists qualified via online poker rooms – two from PartyPoker and two from PokerStars (there's hope for all of us, then).

The following list shows how the prize money for the main event of the WSOP has escalated over the years:

1971 – $30,000
1976 – $220,000
1980 – $385,000
1985 – $700,000
1990 – $805,000
1995 – $1,000,000
2000 – $1,500,000
2002 – $2,000,000
2003 – $2,500,000
2004 – $5,000,000
2005 – $7,500,000

All the tournaments are knock-outs, which is one reason they have proved to be so attractive to the TV channels. The astronomical level of the prize money is another factor.

The winners of the various tournaments are awarded a gold bracelet (which many players value more than the cash prize). The prizes are, typically, in six figures with the first place prize for the 2005 championship setting a new record at $7,500,000.

Poker Resources

As poker is a hugely popular game, there are numerous books, magazines and websites devoted to it. The following is a list of recommended reading matter on this subject.

Books

The Internet is a great resource for poker players. You will find hundreds of sites that provide tips and strategies for all the poker games.

"Theory of Poker" by David Sklansky – this is generally regarded as being the definitive work on poker, and is one that all serious poker players should read. Note that it is not intended for beginners.

"Super/System II" by Doyle Brunson – a recently updated version of a poker classic. Well worth reading for the section on no-limit Texas Hold'em.

"Hold'em Excellence" by Lou Krieger – this book provides an excellent step by step description on how to play each stage of a hand in Texas Hold'em.

"Tournament Poker for Advanced Players" by David Sklansky – one of the best books on tournament play.

Websites

There are several different types of poker software available on the Internet. These include programs that provide analysis, odds and probability statistics, and game simulation. Nearly all these programs can be downloaded in "free trial" versions that allow them to be evaluated. Try a few out.

www.cardplayer.com – this is the website of Card Player magazine, and from here you can access over 100 editions of this popular and informative poker publication.

www.poker1.com – website of the well known poker writer, Mike Caro. Here you will find an extensive range of poker articles and resources.

www.texasholdem-poker.com – a complete resource for the poker player. Strategies, articles, poker tools (odds calculators, for example) are all here.

www.pokerineurope.com – this site is mainly for players in Europe, not surprisingly, and has many articles, details of European tournaments, a shop, and a poker forum.

Poker Forums

www.thepokerforum.com
www.recpoker.com
www.pokerroom.com/pokah

Glossary

A

Advertise – you advertise by adopting a different style of play in order to confuse your opponents. The usual procedure is to play more loosely, so that when you get a good hand opponents are more likely to call your bets, thus putting money in the pot.

Ante – a small forced bet at the beginning of a hand to ensure money goes into the pot. In online games, it is used in Seven-Card Stud.

All-in – when players puts *all* their chips into the pot, they are said to be all-in. This can happen in any game, but is more commonly seen in no-limit games where it is a powerful maneuver.

All-In Protection – a method of protecting your investment in a pot if you lose your connection during the hand and are unable to re-establish the connection before your time to act is up. If you are holding the winning hand, the pot that has accumulated to the point when you timed out (the main pot) will be awarded to you, and the rest (the side pot) will be awarded to the player with the next best hand. Note that due to systematic abuse of this feature, most sites will allow this only once or twice in a 24-hour period.

American Airlines – pocket aces (A-A). Also known as pocket rockets.

B

Backdoor – catching both the turn and the river card to complete a drawing hand, usually a straight or a flush.

Bad Beat – holding a really good hand only to have it beaten by an even better one. A typical example would be a full house being beaten by a four-of-a-kind.

Belly Buster – another term for an inside straight where an inside card is needed to complete the hand, e.g. a K with A-Q-J-T.

Beer Hand – 2-7 off suit: the worst start cards in Texas Hold'em. When you're dealt these, it's time to go and have a beer.

Big Blind – a full-sized forced bet made by the player two places to the left of the dealer button.

Bluff – a bet that is made to try and convince opponents that the player has a much stronger hand than is actually the case.

Board – the community cards: flop, turn, and river.

Boat – a full house.

Bring-in Bet – a forced bet in Stud poker, typically half of the lower betting limit.

Bubble – the last position in a tournament that doesn't earn any money.

C

Call – a bet that matches the previous player's bet.

Calling Station – a player who does little else than call, and rarely folds or raises.

Cap – making the last permitted raise in a betting round, usually the fourth.

Chasing – consistently trying to hit unlikely draws. This is a common error.

Check – an action that keeps a player in the game without actually placing money in the pot. This option is available only when a previous player has also checked.

Check-Raise – checking, and then raising when the betting comes back round. The raise option will only be available, though, if another player has made a bet.

Collusion – a form of cheating, whereby two or more players collude to gain an advantage over the other players. They communicate by telephone or instant messaging to tell each other what their cards are. They will then use this information to gain an unfair advantage. However, online poker rooms have ways of detecting collusion.

Connector – two cards that are next to each other in rank, e.g. 9-8.

Counterfeit – this is when a card that ruins a good hand falls on the board. For example, a player is holding A-9 and the board is 5-6-7-8. The player has a straight. Then the river brings a 9. Now everyone has the same straight. The player's hand has been counterfeited.

Cowboys – a pair of kings (K-K).

D

Dead Card – a card needed by a player to complete a hand, but that is already in play, and thus unavailable.

Dominated Hand – a hand that is similar to another hand but with a lower kicker. For example, A-J dominates A-8 because A-8 needs to improve to at least a pair in order to win. If neither hand improves, A-J will win.

Door Card – the first card dealt face-up in Seven-Card Stud.

Double Up – double your chip stack in one hand. This is usually the result of a successful all-in bet in no-limit Hold'em.

Double-Suited – a term used in Omaha to describe a starting hand that has two suits, e.g. As-Ts-2d-4d.

Drawing Dead – attempting to hit a hand that will lose even if it completes. For example, you have 5-6-7-8 and an opponent has T-J-Q-K. If a 9 comes to complete your straight it will complete a higher straight for your opponent.

Drawing Hand – a hand that needs one or more cards to make a complete hand, e.g. A-2-3 needs 4-5 to complete a straight.

E

Extra Blind – a forced bet made by a player joining a table. The purpose is to prevent players skipping from table to table to avoid paying the blind money.

F

Flat Call – this is when a player calls with a strong hand, instead of raising.

Flop – the first three community cards in Texas Hold'em.

Flush – a five-card hand in which all the cards are the same suit.

Flush Draw – a hand made up of the same suit but needing more cards of that suit to complete a flush.

Fold – the act of discarding a hand.

Four-of-a-Kind – a hand containing four cards of the same rank, e.g. Q-Q-Q-Q. Commonly known as "quads".

Free Card – a card that you haven't had to make a bet to see.

Freeroll – a tournament with no entry fee. These are usually promotions run by poker rooms to attract customers and, also, to tempt them into trying their luck at the real money tournaments.

G

Gutshot Straight – a straight draw that needs an inside card to complete it: e.g. 4-5-7-8, which needs a 6.

H

Heads-Up – a term used to describe a situation when two players are contesting the pot. It is also used to describe a two-seat table.

Hit – a term used when players have caught a card, or the hand, they wanted. For example, "the flop hit" or "you hit your hand".

Hole Cards – the initial cards dealt to a player at the beginning of a hand. Also known as pocket cards and start cards.

I

Implied Odds – a factor used when calculating pot odds to take into account any additional bets that may be made. For example, a player may bet with a drawing hand even though the pot odds don't warrant the bet. The player has calculated that an opponent will call the bet and thus increase the pot odds.

Inside Straight Draw – four cards that need one in the middle to complete a straight. Also known as a gutshot straight.

J

Jackpot – a bonus paid by poker rooms. Examples are a Royal Flush jackpot and a Bad Beat jackpot.

K

Kicker – a card used to determine the winner in a situation when two or more players have the same hand. For example, Player A has 7-7 with an ace kicker and Player B has 7-7 with a queen kicker. Player A has the highest kicker and wins the pot.

L

Limp – a term for a player who enters a pot by calling the bet made by the big blind.

Loose – a style of play adopted by many beginners in which far too many hands are played. Loose players are generally regarded as the easiest ones to beat.

Locked – a hand is said to be locked, or locked up, when it cannot be beaten.

M

Made Hand – a hand that can win without any improvement, i.e. a pair of aces.

Maniac – a very loose and aggressive player who does a lot of raising and bluffing. These players can be dangerous opponents when the luck is with them, but solid players will always beat them eventually.

Miss – the situation when a player has failed to get the card or hand he or she needed.

Muck – to discard a hand without revealing it to opposing players. In a bricks and mortar poker room, the muck is the pile of folded cards on the table.

Multi-way Pot – a pot that is being contested by several players.

N

No-Limit – a variation on the standard form of fixed-limit poker, in which players are not restricted in terms of the size of bet they can make.

Nuts – a hand that cannot be beaten with the board as it stands. The term is also used when a player has the best hand of a particular type, e.g. a nut straight or a nut flush.

O

Off-Suit – a hand containing cards of different suits. For example, 2s-8c.

Omaha – a version of poker in which players are dealt four start cards with five community cards. Hands must be made using two of the start cards and three of the community cards.

One-Gap Connector – two cards that are two ranks apart. For example, K-J is a one-gap connector. 5-2 is a two-gap connector.

Out – this is a card needed by a player to complete a hand. For example, if a ten is needed then there are four outs (four tens in the pack).

Overcard – this is a card higher than any on the board. If you are holding 7-J and the flop is T-8-3 then you have one overcard.

Overpair – a pair that is higher than any board card. If you have T-T and the board cards are 9-3-8, the T-T is an overpair.

P

Paint Card – an ace, king, queen, or jack.

Pocket Cards – a player's face-down cards that opponents cannot see.

Pocket Pair – a pair in a player's pocket cards.

Post – placing a forced bet on the table, e.g. "posting the small blind".

Pot-Limit – a variation of poker in which the maximum bet is restricted to the size of the pot.

Pot Odds – the ratio between the amount of money in the pot and the size of the bet needed to call the previous bet. The figure is used to determine if making a bet is likely to be profitable.

Protecting a Hand – the act of making a bet (a raise, usually) to force opponents to fold.

Q

Quads – a term used to describe a four-of-a-kind, e.g. K-K-K-K.

R

Ragged – community cards that are unlikely to be any good for any player. For example, a flop of 2h-7d-Js is a ragged flop.

Rags – a set of very poor cards that are unplayable.

Raise – calling an opponent's bet and adding another bet to it. In other words, the bet is doubled.

Rainbow – a set of cards of different suits that cannot be made into a flush. A flop of As-Jd-8h is a rainbow flop.

Rake – a percentage of the pot taken by the poker room as its profit.

Rank – the strength of a card or a hand. For example, a king is a high-ranked card and a two is a low-ranked card. A flush is a high-ranked hand while a pair is a low-ranked hand.

Re-Raise – the act of raising a player who has raised previous players.

Represent – an act of deception in which a player attempts to make opponents think he or she has a particular hand. For example, if the flop brings a king, a player who immediately raises would be "representing" a good hand containing at least another king.

Ring Game – any poker game that is not a tournament.

River – the last community card in Texas Hold'em. It is also the final card dealt in Seven-Card Stud.

Rock – this is a term used to describe a very tight player who plays only the best start cards and never raises except when holding a winning hand. These players find it hard to win decent sized pots as they are so predictable. As soon as they make a move, opponents fold.

Runner – a turn or river card that completes a player's hand. If it's both then it becomes a "runner runner", e.g. a runner runner straight.

S

Sandbagging – another term for slow-playing.

Scare Card – a community card that could turn a winning hand into a losing one. For example, a third card of the same suit falling on the board makes a flush a possibility. A player holding a straight would be "scared" by this card.

Semi-Bluff – this is when a player aggressively plays a weak hand that has the potential to become a very strong hand. A flush or straight draw is a typical example. The player hopes that by doing this the other players will fold. However, if they don't, there is still a chance of improving the hand and winning the pot anyway.

Set – another term for a three-of-a-kind.

Short-Stack – a term used when a player is running out of chips, i.e. "short-stacked".

Showdown – the final stage in a hand when all the players still in have their cards turned face-up.

Sidepot – when a player goes all-in, a sidepot is created for other players. The all-in player is eligible only for the main pot.

Sixth Street – the sixth card dealt in Seven-card Stud.

Slow-Playing – an act of deception designed to trick opponents into thinking a player has a poor hand, and thus enticing them to put money in the pot.

Small Blind – the lower of the two blind forced bets. The player immediately to the left of the dealer has to post the small blind.

Smooth-Calling – another term for slow-playing. Instead of raising with a big hand, a player will just call to keep opponents in the game.

Steal the Blinds – the act of raising pre-flop to make everyone fold, and thus take the pot there and then.

Steel Wheel – a straight flush – A-2-3-4-5.

Sucker Straight – also known as "Idiot End". This is when a player has hit the low end of a straight and an opponent has hit the high end.

Suited Connector – connected cards of the same suit, e.g. Ks-Qs.

T

Tell – an indication given unwittingly by a player who has a strong hand that gives the fact away. Online, tells are restricted to the speed at which players act.

Three-Betting – making the third bet in fixed-limit Texas Hold'em. For example, Player A makes a bet and Player B raises. If Player C re-raises, this player is three-betting.

Three-Quarter – this is when a player holds both the best high and the best low hands in a Hi/Lo game. Another player also holding one of these hands can only win a quarter of the pot, and is said to have been "three-quartered".

Tilt – players go on tilt when they lose control of their emotions. In this situation their play becomes irrational, and as a result they lose their stack quickly.

Top Kicker – a hand with the highest possible kicker. For example, a pair of kings with an ace.

Top Pair – a pair containing the highest card on the board. If a player is holding K-9 and the board cards are 8-2-K, the player has the top pair.

Trapping – an act of deception in which a good hand is slow-played to "trap" an opponent into thinking he or she has a better hand.

Trips – another term for a three-of-a-kind.

Turn – the fourth community card in Texas Hold'em and Omaha.

U

Under the Gun – the player to the left of the big blind. This player is the first to act, and is therefore said to be "under the gun".

Underdog – this term describes a player against whom the odds are stacked. Statistically, this player has more chance of losing than of winning.

Underpair – a pair that is lower than any card on the board. For example, a player has 3-3 and the board is showing 6-K-9.

Up-card – a card that is part of a player's hand, which the other players can see. Up-cards are seen in Stud poker.

W

Wheel – a term for the best possible low-hand in Hi/Lo Stud and Hi/Lo Omaha – A-2-3-4-5.

Wrap – in Omaha, a starting hand containing four cards of consecutive rank, e.g. 2-3-4-5.

Z

Zone – a player who's making all the right moves is said to be in the "zone".

Index

Q

R

S